QUESTIONS and ANSWERS about the HOLY SPIRIT

Introduction by Thomas E. Trask
Foreword by David Yonggi Cho

Compiled and Edited by Hal Donaldson,
Ken Horn & Ann Floyd

Pentecostal Evangel Books
Published by Gospel Publishing House
02-3032

Dedicated to Stanley M. Horton for his contributions to our understanding of the person and work of the Holy Spirit.

Special recognition to the staff of the *Pentecostal Evangel*: Randy Clute, Sue Giarratano, Jodi Harmon, Scott Harrup, John W. Kennedy, Ron Kopczick, Kirk Noonan, Ashli O'Connell, Robyn Redmon and Sarah Simmons.

Cover design by Randy Clute

Scripture references are from the King James Version, except as noted.

Library of Congress Control Number 2001 131452
International Standard Book Number 0-88243-303-2
Printed in the United States of America

Contents

■ THE HOLY SPIRIT IN THE CHRISTIAN'S LIFE

APPENDIX

Foreword

The Church is like a sailboat floating on a calm sea. Unless the wind blows, the sailboat will not move. When the Holy Spirit comes, then the Church starts to move. When the wind of the Spirit does not blow, the Church cannot move. The revival for the last days is the revival of the Holy Spirit.

It is not by might, nor by power but by the Spirit of God. To minister for Christ, one should be full of the Holy Spirit. That is the most important criterion.

On the Day of Pentecost, by the power of the Holy Spirit, the powerless disciples became spiritual and became wonderful witnesses to the whole world.

When we are born again, we have the Holy Spirit; but when we are baptized in the Holy Spirit, then we receive a new dimension of power in our lives. We have new fellowship with the Holy Spirit. We should have the baptism in the Holy Spirit according to the Bible.

Many people go ahead of the Holy Spirit. Jesus said that He only did what the Father showed Him to do. We must not go ahead of the Holy Spirit. He is in the active role, and we are in the receptive role. We can change our world through His power.

You are God's precious vessel and He wants to use you for His glorious purposes. It is the intent of this book to help readers become men and women of the Spirit, for the glory of God.

David Yonggi Cho
Pastor, Yoido Full Gospel Church
Seoul, South Korea

Introduction

Jesus instructed believers to tarry in Jerusalem until they were endued ("clothed," NIV) with power from on high (Luke 24:49). They obeyed, and He sent the promise of the Father, the Holy Spirit, upon the Early Church.

The Holy Spirit's empowerment is still available to help men and women accomplish the task of worldwide evangelism. What would have been impossible to do alone is possible with the Holy Spirit's empowerment in His time frame. The empowerment grants supernatural insight into what methods to use to accomplish the task.

The church must remain committed to and dependent upon the power of the Holy Spirit. The church's work is a divine ministry that needs divine equipment. The enduement of power spans cultures, distances, and governments. This enduement is given moment by moment.

The Holy Spirit was not given to please us, but to make us witnesses (Acts 1:8). We enjoy the fullness of the Spirit only as we use it for His work. Only in evangelizing can the church of Jesus Christ realize the meaning of Pentecost.

The Holy Spirit also gives power to receive the life of Christ—power to be, rather than to say or do. Our works and words must come from our inmost being or they will have little power. We must walk the walk before we talk the talk.

One characteristic of the Spirit-filled Early Church was its willingness to sacrifice. From early days men and women made sacrifices. The Holy Spirit placed this in their hearts, minds, and spirits.

God equipped His church with the power of Pentecost to finish the work He gave us to do. Let us not presume upon the past work of the Holy Spirit as did Samson. It is the purpose of this book to encourage us to wait before Him until we have been freshly endued, for that is when we will see the miraculous and God will confirm His Word with signs following. Jesus will be glorified and His church built.

Thomas E. Trask
General Superintendent, Assemblies of God

I.
THE HOLY
SPIRIT IN
HISTORY

1

WHAT IS PENTECOST?

By Paul E. Lowenberg

No treatise of the Holy Spirit at Pentecost is complete unless the origins of this New Testament phenomenon are studied. He is more than just the Third Person of the Trinity. His place in the Church's growth and development goes beyond the doctrinal relationship in the Godhead. The Holy Spirit is sent from the Father; He is obtained from the Father by the Son; He is poured out by the Son (Acts 2:33).

The Spirit who moved upon the face of the waters (Genesis 1:2) moved with power and conviction at Pentecost. Men and women were filled with this Spirit (Acts 2:4). Many were pricked in their hearts and cried out, "What shall we do?" (Acts 2:37).

God's Holy Spirit abides with the believer forever. He is the Comforter (John 14:16,17), the Teacher, the Guide. He is the glorifier of Jesus (John 16:14) and the reprover of men (John 16:8). He empowers men to be witnesses (Acts 1:8). We are sanctified by the Spirit (1 Peter 1:2). God's Word was given through men as they were exercised by the Holy Ghost (2 Peter 1:21). And the Spirit affirms our relationship to Jesus Christ as His children (Romans 8:16).

Considering the Spirit's tremendous and far-reaching ministry, we can better understand Jesus' statement: "It is expedient [to your advantage] ... that I go away: for if I go not away, the Comforter will not come unto you; but if I depart, I will send him unto you" (John 16:7). As long as Jesus was *with* them, the Holy Spirit was not *in* them. Until now they had been observers; now they were to be leaders and witnesses. They had accompanied Him; now they were to go for Him. They had heard Him; now they were to proclaim Him.

On the Day of Pentecost they were now fully authorized to represent the kingdom of God and the King. They were to continue what Jesus had begun.

What is Pentecost? It is more than just the day when God initially poured out the Holy Spirit. It is more than just an experience of the Spirit's baptism.

Pentecost Is a Prayer

Jesus said, "I will pray the Father, and he shall give you another Comforter, that he may abide with you forever" (John 14:16). Jesus knew the men who followed Him—their weaknesses, temperaments, shortcomings, and misguided zeal. In His high priestly prayer He said, "I pray for them" (John 17:9). Only the abiding Spirit could transform these men and make them fit representatives of a new passion, a new Kingdom.

Pentecost Is a Promise

With His disciples on the Mount of Olives just before His ascension, Jesus declared, "Behold, I send the promise of my Father upon you" (Luke 24:49). Earlier He had said, "If ye then, being evil, know how to give good gifts unto your children; how much more shall your heavenly Father give the Holy Spirit to them that ask him?" (Luke 11:13). The Father promised this enrichment. Jesus further promised He personally would fulfill this promise.

Pentecost Is a Prediction

Isaiah prophesied: "I will pour my Spirit upon thy seed, and my blessing upon thine offspring" (Isaiah 44:3). The prophet Zechariah assured Israel that God would come to their aid: "And I will pour upon the house of David ... the spirit of grace and of supplications: and they shall look upon me whom they have pierced" (Zechariah 12:10). While this event may follow the Church Age, which terminates with the rapture of the Church, nevertheless it is one of the major predictions of the Spirit's outpouring.

Joel added a great word: "And it shall come to pass afterward, that I will pour out my Spirit upon all flesh" (Joel 2:28). At the outpouring on the Day of Pentecost, Peter substantiated the dramatic events by quoting Joel's words to the astonished crowd (Acts 2:16). "This is that," Peter announced.

Pentecost Is Power

Jesus promised, "Ye shall receive power, after that the Holy Ghost is come upon you: and ye shall be witnesses" (Acts 1:8). The Greek word *martyres,* translated "witnesses," is used occasionally in the New Testament of those who have witnessed even unto death (Acts 22:20; Revelation 2:13; 17:6). To face the opposition as representatives of Jesus Christ, they would need an inner strength. To conquer their own temptations and to control strong human passions, they would need an enduement of divine power. The weak would need to be strong; the faltering, courageous. The foolish must now be wise; the bashful, bold. The double-minded must become persons of strong convictions. This the Spirit would impart to them.

They must have power to face a cunning and hostile enemy. They must have power to contend uncompromisingly for the faith. They must have power to perform miracles and to preach the Word of God unflinchingly. This power had been accorded to them if they maintained a life filled with the Holy Spirit.

Pentecost Is Praying

Prayer is almost synonymous with the Holy Spirit. Paul exhorted the Ephesians to pray "always with all prayer and supplication in the Spirit" (Ephesians 6:18). Jude likewise encouraged his audience: "Build up yourselves on your most holy faith, praying in the Holy Ghost" (Jude 20).

Praying in the Spirit is the highest order of prayer possible. The preposition *in* indicates location. The believer has moved into the area of the Spirit; he is surrounded by the Spirit; he is wrapped around by the Spirit; he has moved into the Spirit's realm. This is not an in-and-out or off-and-on experience.

Jesus used the word *abide:* "If ye abide in me, and my words abide in you, ye shall ask what ye will, and it shall be done unto you" (John 15:7). So many prayers are not answered because people have not learned to abide in Christ, to pray in the Spirit.

Paul added a further enlightening word in Romans 8:26: "Likewise the Spirit also helpeth our infirmities: for we know not what we should pray for as we ought: but the Spirit itself maketh intercession for us with groanings which cannot be uttered."

What a startling and humiliating discovery—"we know not what we should pray for." Our own unspirituality overwhelms us. But we have a Helper. He puts utterance to our sighs, words to our groanings, and prays out His will through us.

It was 1951. I was leaving Japan. We had started a church in Osaka. My flight back to Shreveport, Louisiana, was scheduled. The closer the time came for my flight, the more disturbed and restless I became about flying on this particular airline. I tried to secure an alternate flight but was told there were no vacancies on any airline out of Japan for 30 days. Feeling so sure I must not fly the first airline, I resigned myself to wait the 30 extra days. Yet six hours later I had a seat on another airline.

Arriving in San Francisco I learned the first flight had crashed on an island in the Aleutians.

My father in Canada was disturbed about my safety, though he knew absolutely nothing about my dilemma. Moved by the Holy Spirit he gave himself to prayer in the Spirit. He literally prayed me off one plane onto another so I could come back to my family and ministry.

Pentecost Is Purging

The purpose of Christ's coming to earth was to secure a Bride who would be without spot or wrinkle or any such thing (Ephesians 5:27). The Hebrews letter urges believers to "follow peace with all men, and holiness, without which no man shall see the Lord" (12:14). The Holy Spirit is to make men holy. We are to partake of His holiness (Hebrews 12:10) and perfect holiness in the fear of God (2 Corinthians 7:1).

Sin was judged severely in the Early Church. Ananias and Sapphira died for their duplicity (Acts 5:1-11). Elymas the sorcerer was struck blind for opposing Paul's testimony to Sergius Paulus, a Roman deputy (Acts 13:6-12). John the Baptist had predicted earlier that Jesus would baptize with the Holy Ghost and fire (Luke 3:16). Fire purifies, cleanses, purges.

Pentecost Is Preaching

Pentecost produced instant preachers. The disciples preached with eloquence and authority, using Old Testament truths to support the message of Christ's death and resurrection. A few days before they had disappeared in the shadows and forsaken their Lord when He needed them most. Now they confronted those same authorities: "Ye have taken, and by wicked hands have crucified and slain [him]" (Acts 2:22,23). The only answer to this radical transformation is the infilling of the Holy Spirit—the Spirit of Christ resurrected.

In Acts 4 we read that the apostles were arrested and brought before the Sanhedrin. "Then Peter, filled with the Holy Ghost ..." (v.8). We must assume it was a fresh infilling, subsequent to Pentecost. In the prayer meeting that followed it is again recorded, "They were all filled with the Holy Ghost, and they spake the word of God with boldness" (Acts 4:31). In each case the filling of the Spirit was followed by inspired and convincing preaching.

In the Nazareth synagogue Jesus said, "The Spirit of the Lord is upon me, because he hath anointed me to preach"

(Luke 4:18). In His post-Resurrection meeting with His disciples He said, "Go ye into all the world, and preach the gospel" (Mark 16:15). Paul's last charge to Timothy was, "Preach the word" (2 Timothy 4:2).

Pentecost is preaching—anointed preaching, gracious preaching, inspired preaching, intelligent preaching, sincere preaching. It is preaching the grace of God, the love of God, the power and mercies of God, the judgments of God, and the blessed hope that God holds out to all men everywhere.

Pentecost is God's final answer to the last day of lukewarmness and falling away. Pentecost is hearts aflame, lives totally dedicated, motivated by a burning passion to preach Christ and Him crucified to our world before He comes again to set up His great, everlasting kingdom.

No wonder we need to be filled with the Spirit.

Paul E. Lowenberg, D.D., is a former executive presbyter of the Assemblies of God. He lives in Wichita, Kansas.

2

WHAT HAPPENED AFTER THE DAY OF PENTECOST?

By Kenneth D. Barney

The Day of Pentecost impacted Jerusalem. Jesus' enemies thought they were rid of Him. Suddenly their dreams were shattered.

Apostate religious leaders and heathen government officials realized they had a new force on their hands. An insignificant group of 120 suddenly grew to 3,120. All were declaring Jesus was alive.

Joel prophesied, "It shall come to pass" (Joel 3:18). Now it had come to pass. Jesus promised, "When he is come" (John 16:8). Now He had come. He had come to live in Christ's followers, not merely to empower them for a brief mission. "Another Comforter, that he may abide with you for ever"—that is what Jesus said (John 14:16).

What adjective can do justice to the events of those hours?

But what about the next day, the day after Pentecost? Was everything over with the sunset? Did the revival subside in a few hours? Was the tremendous spiritual surge followed by a receding tide that never returned? No. The true quality of Pentecost was demonstrated by what hap-

17

pened the next day, and the weeks, months, and years following.

Let the record speak for itself: "And they, continuing daily with one accord in the temple, and breaking bread from house to house, did eat their meat with gladness and singleness of heart, praising God, and having favor with all the people. And the Lord added to the church daily such as should be saved" (Acts 2:46,47).

What value can be placed on a Pentecost that has nothing left after the first thrill has subsided? Pentecost is not a one-shot spiritual high. It is not a euphoria that exhausts itself without leaving permanent effects.

What remains after the high makes Pentecost what God intended it to be. As we follow the Early Church's ministry in the Book of Acts, qualities emerge which show the permanence of the Pentecostal experience. What was true then is a pattern for the church today. It must be if we are to fulfill our calling and mission.

Pentecost brought a level of spiritual life unattainable by human effort

Acts 9:31 says Jesus' followers were "walking in the fear of the Lord, and in the comfort of the Holy Ghost." This was the norm now, not the exception. Spirit-filled believers found a new way to walk. No longer did they strain to obey a Law inscribed in stone. The Spirit brought the Law to the interior of every life, and the world saw the results daily.

I remember the first Pentecostal service I attended. I had been saved for several years, yet in that little country congregation I felt spiritual vigor. I recognized the source of what I felt was the uninhibited flow of the Spirit through those Christians.

People would speak of "being in Pentecost." Someone would ask, "How long have you been in Pentecost?" The answers might be, "I've been in Pentecost 10 years," or "I've been in Pentecost nearly all my life." Obviously they weren't talking about a denomination; they were describing a way of life.

Pentecost brought the operation
of the spiritual gifts

These must not be confused with natural abilities and talents. The Spirit's gifts are His supernatural operations through individuals to meet needs.

Paul compared the church to a human body. Each part has a function to perform for the well-being of the whole. Hands reach out to perform the activities. Feet provide mobility. Eyes and ears gather information and transmit it to the brain for evaluation. These members also detect danger.

The gifts of the Spirit have much the same function in the church. The church needs knowledge and direction, awareness of danger, and protection from enemies. The church must distinguish between what is deadly and what is wholesome, between the false and the true. It must understand God's plan and purpose.

Although we see manifestations of gifts in the Old Testament (healings, miracles, and prophecy), they were usually associated with chosen individuals. Most were prophets.

Only after Pentecost did the whole range of spiritual gifts begin to be exercised through all of God's people who were baptized in the Spirit. Paul said these manifestations are "given to every man," referring to every Spirit-filled believer (1 Corinthians 12:7).

In the Book of Acts after Pentecost, we observe needs arising in the church's life. We also note how the Spirit's timely exercise of the appropriate gifts met those needs. This is a vital part of the permanent effects of Pentecost. In these days of fierce spiritual conflict they must be part of the church's weapons.

Pentecost energized the Church into
a dynamic force

Christ's followers did not merely react when the world acted. The opposite was true. After Pentecost the world knew the church was in town. Everyone was familiar with religion, but something new had burst on the scene. The sharp distinction between the church and its surroundings always stuck in the world's face. They had a problem on their hands too big to handle.

Someone has said the early Christians preached like people who had just seen the risen Christ. A few of them had seen Him; the majority had not. Yet the Spirit had made Him just as real to them.

Today's society needs to hear from Christians who live and speak as if they have just come from an audience with the risen Lord. The Spirit's presence and power will make us a people who leave that kind of impression on the world.

Pentecost must become to all of us more than just a past experience to which we pay lip service. That experience must be an unbroken reality that intensifies rather than fades with the passing of time. Then our world will know the Church is alive in this world.

Kenneth D. Barney, an Assemblies of God minister, was adult editor in the Sunday School Curriculum and Literature Department at the Assemblies of God Headquarters before his retirement. He lives in Springfield, Missouri.

3

WHERE DID MODERN PENTECOSTALISM BEGIN?

By Gary B. McGee

How can the world be evangelized in the 'last days' before the soon return of Christ?" asked many Christians at the turn of the 20th century. Thousands of missionaries served abroad, millions of dollars had been invested, but the number of Protestant converts had only reached 3.6 million out of a world population of 1.5 billion. Jesus had said, "This gospel of the kingdom shall be preached in all the world for a witness unto all nations; and then shall the end come" (Matthew 24:14). What was the divine plan?

Many evangelicals, both at home and on the mission field, had been praying for the outpouring of the Spirit as predicted by the prophet Joel (2:28-32). Many also discovered the scriptural promises of physical healing (Isaiah 53:4,5; James 5:13-16). With the growing belief that the world would go from bad to worse before Christ's return, radical evangelicals now believed that only the supernatural outpouring of the Spirit could save the day. Indeed, only evangelism with the demonstration of the Spirit's power in "signs and wonders" (Acts 5:12) could complete the Great Commission.

Among many who sought for a special baptism of power were seven celebrated English athletes known as the "Cambridge Seven." They arrived in China in 1885 to serve as missionaries with J. Hudson Taylor's China Inland Mission. Three of them, including C.T. Studd, prayed for the "Pentecostal" gift of the Mandarin language according to the promise of Mark 16:17, "they shall speak with new tongues." When criticized, they returned to their language books.

Years later, Charles F. Parham encouraged students at his Bethel Bible School in Topeka, Kansas, to pray for the gift of tongues. He had been inspired by the spiritual dynamics of the New Testament church as recorded in the Book of Acts. Along with his students (Agnes Ozman was the first), he was baptized in the Spirit and spoke in tongues in early January 1901.

An independent preacher in the Wesleyan-Holiness movement, he forged his most enduring legacy by noting that tongues marks the "Bible evidence" of Spirit baptism in the Book of Acts, later referred to by Pentecostals as the "initial evidence."

The years immediately following the Topeka revival proved discouraging. Biting criticisms from newspapers and individuals, the death of his infant son, and the loss of the Bible school property wounded Parham deeply. Nevertheless, he rose above these depressing circumstances and his message of the Pentecostal baptism gradually gained more acceptance.

A revival outside Houston, Texas, in 1905 led him to open another Bible school there. One of his students, William J. Seymour, was to play a key role in events that followed on Azusa Street in Los Angeles.

In the summer of 1906, several holiness believers in South India were baptized in the Spirit and spoke in tongues. It appears they were completely unaware of the happenings at

Topeka and Azusa Street. Thus, the Holy Spirit fell in the East as well.

It was from Azusa that Pentecostal missionaries first left for the mission lands. But much to their disappointment, they soon discovered that speaking in tongues did not enable them to bypass language school. Closer examination of the Scriptures made them realize that "glossolalia" usually meant praying in unknown tongues.

One such missionary, A.G. Garr, found upon arriving in Calcutta, India, that he had not received the Bengali language after all. He then wrote in March 1907 that praying in tongues represents "the sweetest joy and the greatest pleasure to the soul when God comes upon one ... and begins himself to speak His language. Oh, the blessedness of His presence when those foreign words flow from the Spirit of God through the soul and then are given back to Him in prayer, in prophecy or in worship." Pentecostals now came to better understand speaking in tongues as prayer in the Spirit, the means of spiritual empowerment.

Over the years, the linkage of Spirit baptism and glossolalia with evangelism in "signs and wonders" changed the landscape of Christianity. In looking back, little could that band of humble seekers at Parham's Topeka Bible school have realized that Pentecostalism in its various forms would someday prove to be the most dynamic force of the century for evangelization.

Gary B. McGee, Ph.D., is professor of church history at Assemblies of God Theological Seminary in Springfield, Missouri.

4

WHAT IS THE SIGNIFICANCE OF THE AZUSA STREET REVIVAL?

By Ken Horn

I t was an old abandoned building on a run-down street. It had last served as a livery stable—before that, a ware-house. Just an old "tumbled-down shack." But it became the tabernacle of the Lord's presence to people hungry for the glory of God.

Pentecost hadn't stopped in Kansas. In 1905, Charles Parham opened a Bible school in Houston, Texas. An African-American believer named William J. Seymour eagerly received the teachings there regarding the fullness of the Holy Spirit.

Earlier, a Baptist pastor in California, Joseph Smale, had heard of a tremendous revival occurring in Wales under Evan Roberts. Smale went there and Roberts encouraged him to seek such a revival in Los Angeles. When Smale returned, he instituted prayer meetings. Other similar prayer meetings began to break out in the area. While California believers prayed for a mighty move of God, the humble

Seymour sat in Texas learning about the ways of the Holy Spirit.

Next, God orchestrated a divine appointment that would launch the fledgling movement to unprecedented heights. A woman from one of the California groups met Seymour in Houston and was impressed by his godliness. On her recommendation, Seymour was invited to pastor in Los Angeles. He accepted. But he preached about a fullness of the Holy Spirit accompanied by tongues. This message was foreign to his hearers' ears. Thus, though many accepted the teaching, he was locked out of the church. He moved to a private home on Bonnie Brae Street to preach.

Here, on April 9, 1906, seven worshipers were struck by the power of God and began to speak in other tongues. Soon people of all races and from a rich variety of church backgrounds were attracted—and many spoke in tongues. It initially produced a movement that was color-blind. Soon word spread and the Bonnie Brae house was too small.

The meetings moved to an old building that had originally been an African Methodist Episcopal church at 312 Azusa Street. This became the home of the revival. People visited the Apostolic Faith Gospel Mission there in large numbers. There was continuous revival for three years. It was not uncommon for a meeting to go from 10 a.m. until midnight.

Yet there were none of the trappings often associated with a large revival. In this, Azusa was much like its overseas companion, the Welsh revival. Organization was minimal and there was no advertising. Offerings were never taken, but could be left at the door. Spontaneity was the unofficial order of service. Even the messages were generally spontaneous. When the sermon was completed, the altars were opened and people flooded to them. Witnesses marveled that preaching so simple was attended by a power so great. As the Spirit moved, people would "fall prostrate under the power of God." They often got up speaking in tongues—with lives dramatically transformed.

But the movement did not exalt tongues. Seymour set the tone for Pentecostal doctrine early on when he said, "Now, don't go from this meeting and talk about tongues, but try to get people saved." He preached that a power for service could be found in the baptism in the Holy Ghost and fire—and that tongues would surely follow this Baptism.

Though there were some excesses found at Azusa Street, the move of God there changed people significantly. A tremendous conviction of sin turned people to Christ. It brought unbelievers and backsliders to the Cross, worldly Christians to a deeper walk, and those who were seeking more of God much of the Holy Spirit.

The significance of the Azusa revival cannot be measured by a span of three years or the seemingly local scope of the renewal. The revival influenced people from all over the world. They came and went, taking the fire of Pentecost with them—to Chicago, New York City, Oregon and throughout the United States, to England, Norway, Sweden, and other countries. Gaston B. Cashwell returned to Dunn, North Carolina, where, in January 1907, a revival occurred that became the "Azusa of the South." Through his ministry several existing holiness bodies became Pentecostal, including the Church of God (Cleveland, Tennessee), the Fire-Baptized Holiness Church and the Pentecostal Free-Will Baptist Church. Soon the movement was multiplying itself from new revival centers. From these humble beginnings the Pentecostal movement would spread around the world. It is remarkable that, in a day of prejudice, God used a small place and a humble black preacher to help open the church's eyes to the bigness of God and the power of the Holy Spirit.

The tabernacle was eventually torn down. You can find no trace of the physical building today. But you can still find its spiritual imprint—not just in Los Angeles, but in virtually every corner of the globe.

Ken Horn, D.Min., is managing editor for the *Pentecostal Evangel*.

5

HOW WAS THE ASSEMBLIES OF GOD BORN?

By William W. Menzies

The Assemblies of God came into being at the first General Council, April 6-12, 1914, in Hot Springs, Arkansas. The December 20, 1913, issue of *The Word and Witness*, a periodical edited by E.N. Bell in Malvern, Arkansas, issued a formal call for a "General convention of Pentecostal saints and churches of God in Christ." Despite heated controversy among Pentecostal believers over the issue of forming an organization, the Hot Springs convention brought representatives from many parts of the United States, as well as several foreign countries. More than 300 people attended these historic meetings, of whom 128 officially registered. The roster lists many of the great leaders of the earliest days of the 20th-century Pentecostal movement. It was here that a unanimous resolution was adopted to form a voluntary, cooperative fellowship of Pentecostal churches to be called the General Council of the Assemblies of God.

The 1914 Hot Springs meeting was not the first attempt to gather Pentecostal believers together. Between 1905 and 1913, a variety of camp meetings and conferences were held, chiefly in the south-central United States, with as many as 15 of these gatherings publicized by the summer of 1913.

Some regional associations developed. Short-term Bible institutes were conducted by respected leaders like D.C.O. Opperman to train young preachers. A flurry of periodicals appeared between 1901 and the gathering in 1914 in Hot Springs. These publications helped to give a sense of unity of purpose to the fledgling revival movement and pointed in the direction of a more formal organization.

What caused these early independent Pentecostals to agree to unite to form a new organization? Here are at least four reasons.

Fellowship

Although there were isolated episodes of Pentecostal revival prior to this time, it was in Topeka, Kansas, in 1901, that the Pentecostal experience was given its first theological identity: a belief in a baptism in the Spirit accompanied by the biblical sign of speaking in other tongues, subsequent to new birth. The teaching of a baptism in the Spirit as an enduement of power for witnessing was commonly taught among evangelicals by the 1890s. Pentecostals possessed an expectation that tongues—and other manifestations of the Spirit listed in the New Testament—could be experienced today. This understanding was a cause of great controversy among Christians. Pentecostals were virtually cut off from fellowship with other believers. They felt the need for a new fellowship sharing common faith.

Discipline

A widespread tendency for clusters of Pentecostal believers to gravitate to strong leaders produced a divisive, and even contentious, spirit among some Pentecostals. More mature leaders were uneasy about the splintering effect this personality-centered loyalty was producing. Some of these local leaders were guilty of various abuses, some more serious than others. It became apparent that a means for disciplining leadership was going to be required if the good name of responsible churches was to be preserved. Standards of conduct and practice were needed.

Doctrine

There was a felt need for doctrinal harmony. Many of the early Pentecostal preachers were untrained, lacking an adequate biblical foundation for feeding the flock of God. Enthusiasm was not always matched by wisdom. Some allowed personal experience to govern their teaching. This often created a bewildering assortment of conflicting teachings that led to division and confusion. A precise doctrinal statement was not shaped at this initial General Council, but by 1916 doctrinal controversy precipitated the need for a "Statement of Fundamental Truths," incorporating the salient points of Assemblies of God teaching.

Missions

From the earliest days of the Pentecostal revival, a common thread in the various assemblies was a widespread response to reach the lost for Christ, not only at home, but abroad. Foreign missions and pioneer domestic ministry were high priorities among these early believers. It became apparent very quickly that local churches were not very good foreign missions agencies. The need for correlating foreign work, arranging for forwarding funds to the foreign field, legal representation with foreign governments, and the need for endorsement for holding of mission properties in foreign lands, all pointed toward the need for a more centralized missions enterprise. Stories of missionaries abandoned in isolation on lonely mission fields fueled the sense of urgency. The desire to formulate a more cohesive strategy for sending and supporting missionaries was clearly one of the principal reasons Pentecostalists shed their independent ways to form a cooperative fellowship. From the beginning, the Assemblies of God has been strongly committed to world evangelization.

William W. Menzies, Ph.D., an Assemblies of God missionary, is chancellor of Asia Pacific Theological Seminary in Baguio City, Philippines.

II.
THE HOLY SPIRIT IN GOD'S WORD

6

WHY SHOULD A PERSON SEEK THE INFILLING OF THE SPIRIT?

By George Holmes

It's an order: "Be filled with the Spirit" (Ephesians 5:18). What a happy command. It's like saying to a sick person, "Be filled with health." Or to struggling parents with a large family, "Here's a million dollars." Or to an exhausted couple, "Be renewed with an all-expenses-paid Caribbean cruise."

"Be filled with the Spirit." This is God's level for our living or dying, working or worshiping, walking or waiting. As a command it offers delightful possibilities and a peak experience. Note the ascent. Being born again is a phenomenal and essential spiritual experience. You thus become a new creation in Christ. You enter the kingdom of God. You are totally alive in spirit, soul, and body.

Next, being baptized by the Spirit into Christ's church brings you into union with every member of that organism. You are grafted, spiritually transplanted, into the body of Christ.

And being baptized *in* the Spirit by Jesus Christ graces you for a new order of activity in the spiritual realm. By this spiritual enduement you become an anointed witness for God.

But being filled *with* the Spirit is an ongoing experience of living in a state of spiritual fullness—at any one moment. You overflow like a vessel under a gushing faucet.

Peter was interrogated by the Jewish Supreme Court. The court wanted to know by what power or name he had brought healing to a lame man. Peter on the Day of Pentecost had been baptized in the Holy Spirit. But as he answered his inquisitors, he was "filled [i.e., with a fresh filling] with the Holy Ghost" (Acts 4:8). As his fearless explanation boldly poured forth, the Holy Spirit was filling him, keeping him filled and putting a sharp edge on his words.

Again, being filled with the Spirit was one of the criteria for choosing the seven who administered the funds for the widows. One chosen was Stephen, "a man full of faith and of the Holy Ghost" (Acts 6:5). It was as recognizable a condition as, for instance, being "drunk with wine," with which it is contrasted.

Being filled with the Spirit exhilarates, lifts, and keeps a person in tune with spiritual reality. He is able to perceive eternal things. He has means of interaction with a holy God; in fact, God is residing in his spirit. As a recognizable condition it is authenticated. For instance, the Spirit-filled "walk circumspectly, not as fools, but as wise" (Ephesians 5:15). While filled they are less prone to stumble or make foolish judgments. They are held in balance.

They are also kept from wasting time on trivial pursuits because the things of God's kingdom are kept in bright focus. Christians make the most of every opportunity.

Husbands and wives keeping filled with the Spirit are better able to understand and follow God's plans for their marriage (vv.22-25). The difference this makes is easily recognizable. Likewise, homes and families function more sweetly and are administered in a godly way where parents and children are "filled with the Spirit" (Ephesians 6:1-4). The same can be said of business relationships (6:5-9).

Through the aridity of Egypt flows a stream of life: the river Nile. At certain seasons it overflows and inundates the surrounding desert. Since water is imperative, distant farmers cut ditches to the overflow and bring the water to their own fields. Thus the land is irrigated. In like manner, the rich fullness of the Spirit in our hearts overflows into all our relationships and activities. We become channels bringing the sweetness and power of the Spirit into our homes, churches, countries, and the world.

Prayers gain momentum when we are filled with the Spirit. At the start of each day we need an overflowing refilling. Prayer so often is the connection that brings this to us. Without it our intercessions can become drudgery. Additionally our worship will fall flat unless we are filled with the Spirit because "God is a Spirit: and they that worship him must worship him in spirit and in truth" (John 4:24). Such worship flows from a heart filled with wonder, love, and praise; a heart stirred by the Paraclete and the revelations He brings. It is bowing down in reverence before our Creator, Father, and Lord. It is waiting upon God, embracing God, listening to God. The worship experience, however, is not specifically for our benefit, but because of God's desire to be worshiped. He seeks such worshipers.

Being filled with the Spirit brings our inner receptors into tune with the Almighty; so if and when He speaks, we shall hear and understand His thoughts and desires. Such communications may be for us personally, or they may be given to us to deliver to the church. The Head does speak to the Body through His Spirit actuating a member.

Joy, praise, and harmony are brought about by keeping filled with the Spirit. A delightful church is pictured in Ephesians 5:19-21 (*Living Bible*): "Talk with each other much about the Lord [this will obviate scandal and gossip], quoting psalms and hymns and singing sacred songs [these are much more edifying than the blues of the world], making music in your hearts to the Lord [even the tone deaf can do this when filled with the Spirit]. Always give thanks for everything to our God and Father in the name of our Lord Jesus Christ. Honor Christ by submitting to each other." Problems will be few among such a healthy people.

The list goes on. The blessings multiply. Potential rises.

Being filled with the Spirit will enable us to receive God's revelation of himself. Who knows God? Can He be known? How can He be known—not as a force or a mythical image like Mother Nature or Father Time—but as a true, real, living, loving Being?

Here are some answers from 1 Corinthians 2 (*Living Bible*):

"No one can know God's thoughts except God's own Spirit. And God has actually given us His Spirit (not the world's spirit) to tell us. ... But the man who isn't a Christian can't understand and can't accept these thoughts from God, which the Holy Spirit teaches us. They sound foolish to him, because only those who have the Holy Spirit within them can understand what the Holy Spirit means. ... We Christians actually do have within us a portion of the very thoughts and mind of Christ" (vv.11,12,14,16).

The only way, therefore, that God can be known—experienced—is through the agency of the Holy Spirit. Those filled with the Spirit can receive and understand this revelation. It becomes more glorious as the believer remains filled with the Spirit, for "no mere man has ever seen, heard or even imagined what wonderful things God has ready for those who love the Lord" (1 Corinthians 2:9, *Living Bible*).

You would think every Christian would see the reasonableness of the command to be filled with the Spirit, but many of us seem to live more after the flesh than the Spirit.

This doesn't have to be, if we will yield to God. The seeking to be filled, the need to remain filled lift us out of a listless routine into a constant soaring upward. Then as we minister, pray, worship, and serve others, we shall be kept filled with the Spirit.

George Holmes (1913-99) was an Assemblies of God minister.

7

WHAT IS THE INITIAL PHYSICAL EVIDENCE?

By Watson Argue Sr.

The baptism in the Holy Spirit is a definite experience. When the Spirit of the Lord fills you, you will know it without a doubt.

The Book of Acts records five references of how people received the baptism in the Holy Spirit.

The first record of any receiving the baptism in the Holy Spirit is Acts 2:4: "And they were all filled with the Holy Ghost, and began to speak with other tongues, as the Spirit gave them utterance." We see here that the first thing that happened after they were filled with the Spirit was that they began to speak with other tongues as the Spirit gave them utterance. This is mentioned as the initial evidence.

In Hebrews 8:5 we read, "See ... that thou make all things according to the pattern showed to thee in the mount." We believe Acts 2:4 to be the pattern in the New Testament of how to receive the baptism in the Spirit, and we believe it is our privilege to receive the Baptism according to this pattern.

In Acts 10:44,46, we see how the first company of Gentiles received this experience. Peter was preaching at the house of

Cornelius; and "while Peter yet spake these words, the Holy Ghost fell on all them which heard the word." How did they know they had received the Holy Spirit? "For they heard them speak with tongues, and magnify God." They had the same initial evidence as did those who received on the Day of Pentecost.

In Acts 19:6, we find the first record of anyone's receiving the Baptism under the ministry of Paul: "And when Paul had laid his hands upon them, the Holy Ghost came on them: and they spake with tongues, and prophesied."

We see that the first company of Jews receiving the Baptism, the first record of Gentiles receiving the Baptism, and the first ones to receive the Baptism under the ministry of Paul all spoke with tongues.

Acts 8 tells of the great revival at Samaria. Verses 14 and 15 record that Peter and John were sent to Samaria to help those who had received the Word to receive the Holy Ghost. Verse 17 says, "Then laid they their hands on them, and they received the Holy Ghost." Who were Peter and John? According to Acts 1, Peter and John were two of the 120, and we know that all of the 120 received the Baptism with the evidence of speaking with tongues. These were two Pentecostal preachers who went to Samaria to help these converts receive the Baptism. Since Peter and John had received the Baptism with the evidence of speaking with tongues, surely they would believe and pray until these new converts received the same experience.

"And when Simon saw that through laying on of the apostles' hands the Holy Ghost was given, he offered them money, saying, Give me also this power, that on whomsoever I lay hands, he may receive the Holy Ghost" (Acts 8:18). Something attracted the attention of Simon and so convinced him that he was willing to pay to receive the power that Peter and John had. Undoubtedly the speaking with tongues was what attracted his attention and convinced him.

Our last reference is in Acts 9. Here we read of Saul's going to Damascus to persecute the Christians. On the way he is blinded and falls to the earth as a bright light shines from heaven. He is convicted of his sins and has to be led into the city. While he is there in his blinded condition, praying to the Lord, God speaks to Ananias, telling him to go to Saul and lay hands upon him that he might receive his sight and be filled with the Holy Ghost (v.17).

Ananias did as the Lord instructed. He laid his hands upon Saul for that twofold purpose—that he might receive his sight and be filled with the Holy Ghost. Undoubtedly this is the time and the place when Saul received the Baptism. The Scripture does not record it elsewhere; and, when Ananias was sent for that express purpose and he did his part, surely God would be faithful and do His. Nothing is said about Saul's speaking with tongues.

But we know he did speak with tongues. Saul became known as Paul. He said in 1 Corinthians 14:18, "I thank my God, I speak with tongues more than ye all." If it was not necessary to mention it in Acts 9—but we see that Paul did speak with tongues—it was not necessary to mention it in the account of the revival at Samaria in Acts 8. No doubt the same sign was given to believers there.

I remind those seeking the Baptism: "Ask, and it shall be given you; seek, and ye shall find; knock, and it shall be opened unto you" (Matthew 7:7). Ask—how long? We believe we should keep on asking until we receive. Seek—how long? Until we find. And the same applies to knocking. Keep on knocking until the door of blessing is opened. Some go to the prayer room to tarry and they knock, but not long enough. After knocking about 10 minutes they start thinking about the early hour they have to get up in the morning, and they stop knocking and go home to bed. And about the time they get home, maybe the Baptizer is there to fill them and they miss the blessing.

If you were comfortably settled in bed after a hard day's work, and there came just a little knock at your door, chances are you would never hear it, and never disturb yourself. But if someone started some real knocking and kept it up, you would soon hear it and realize that you would not have any rest until you opened the door and found out what was wanted. So in receiving the baptism in the Spirit, if you don't show that you are really eager to receive, the Lord may not bother to fill you. But if you will just put yourself on the Lord's doorstep, so to speak, and knock and keep on knocking, the Lord will soon see that you will not take no for an answer.

Watson Argue Sr. (1904-85) was a pastor and evangelist. He was the son of A.H. Argue, a pioneer in the Pentecostal Assemblies of Canada.

8

HOW DOES THE HOLY SPIRIT IMPACT A PERSON'S LIFE?

By Zelma Argue

From the first heart wooings of conviction to the final triumph—being caught up to meet the Lord in the air—all God's blessings are ministered to us by the Holy Spirit. Yet the baptism in the Holy Spirit is a distinct experience, as clear-cut, as outstanding, as unmistakable as being baptized in water.

Many people say, "I have felt the presence of the Holy Spirit many times; therefore, I am sure I have the Baptism." No, the presence of the Holy Spirit is not the Baptism.

I was a guest in the home of a dear Christian woman. Her husband was not a Christian. "Do pray for my husband that he might be saved," was her constant request. So we prayed. Many were being saved in the services. Her husband came several times to the revival services, but did not go forward. Then his working hours were changed to nights. We kept praying.

One day he lost his hat. He and his wife looked everywhere but could find no trace of the hat. On the third day his wife found it in the coal bin. When he came home, she showed it to him and told him where she had found it. With an embarrassed smile he said, "I'm going to tell you how it must have gotten there. When my hours were changed to the evening shift at work, I thought I would escape the revival. But I could not get away from it. Three days ago, when down in the basement fixing the furnace, I decided to face the question once for all. So down in the coal bin I took off my hat and started to pray. Ever since I have been earnestly looking to God, and now I know I am saved. I am just waiting for Sunday morning service to tell everyone what Jesus has done for me."

That was the work of the Holy Spirit to convict and save, but the Baptism is beyond this.

Sanctification is not the Baptism. In His last talk with His disciples in the Upper Room, just before the Last Supper, Jesus said, "Now ye are clean through the word which I have spoken unto you" (John 15:3).

Weeks after that, on the day of His ascension from Mount Olivet, He commanded them to tarry at Jerusalem until they were endued with power from on high—until they received the promise of the Father, the Holy Spirit.

To be baptized is to be immersed; that is, to go completely under. Some may be satisfied to receive a sprinkling of the blessing and call that the Baptism, but to be baptized in the Holy Spirit is something deeper than that.

Inward

In Palestine when a man bought a piece of land, he was given a small amount of dirt from the land as tangible assurance that the property was now his. The buyer of the land could not take his purchased possession with him, but he could take the small sample or earnest. Ephesians 1:14 says the Holy Spirit is "the earnest of our inheritance." This experience which Jesus called "the promise of my Father" is the earnest of our inheritance (Luke 24:49). It is a token of the glory that shall be ours. This is the inward purpose of the baptism in the Holy Spirit.

Outward

But this Baptism is not given merely to make us happy. The last words heard from Jesus' lips before He was taken away addressed this: "Ye shall receive power when the Holy Spirit is come upon you: and ye shall be my witnesses both in Jerusalem, and in all Judea and Samaria, and unto the uttermost part of the earth" (Acts 1:8, ASV). In the will of the Lord these two—power and witnessing—are not divorced.

The boiler of a powerful locomotive is filled with water and ready to go. The fire is burning very hot. Someone touches the valve for the whistle. But the engineer does not let all the steam go out through the whistle. Instead he starts a pull, and the engine goes slowly, steadily, surely, as its power tugs at the series of coaches. Gradually it gains greater speed until the power of the steam, produced by the fire and the water, carries the passengers safely to their destinations.

The Christian, endued with the power of the Holy Spirit, will not let it all go out through noisy manifestations, but will use that God-given power to draw men and women to Jesus. He will use that power until souls are led safely home.

Upward

At Christ's tomb a stone was rolled against the entrance. The seal of the Roman government was placed on the tomb, so the stone could not be taken away without breaking the seal. No earthly power dared tamper with what the Roman government had thus sealed.

The apostle Paul speaks of the Holy Spirit, "whereby ye are sealed unto the day of redemption" (Ephesians 4:30). It is a sign placed on the property of the Lord and means, "Hands off." It is keeping power, quickening power, power that raised Jesus from the dead, power that will lift us when

Jesus comes. It is a preservative to protect the fruit of the Lord, a guard against the contaminating influences of the world.

As I was praying, "Lord, make me an instrument in Thy hands that You can use," my mind flashed to a picture of my own instrument, my trombone. As I knelt there, I thought of how I prepared my trombone for use. I run pure, clean water through it to make sure it is clean, inside and out.

Then it seemed the Lord asked, "Is that all?"

"No, Lord," I said. "If I used it then, there would be friction and strain and unnecessary wear on the instrument. After it is clean, I pour on the oil. Then the friction is gone. After it is oiled, just a breath, just a touch, and it responds perfectly." The instrument must first be washed and cleansed. Then it needs oil.

The Lord wants to pour the oil of the Holy Spirit on you. Then, when the oil is there in abundance, He can use the instrument. A whisper from the Lord, a touch, His breath upon you, and you—His chosen instrument—will respond to the Master's will.

Zelma Argue (1900-80) was an Assemblies of God minister, missionary, and evangelist.

9

ARE YOU DISAPPOINTED WITH YOUR SPIRIT BAPTISM?

By C.L. Strom

Is it possible to be baptized—but disappointed? The word "baptize," as used here, refers to what John the Baptist said when speaking of Jesus: "He shall baptize you with the Holy Ghost" (Matthew 3:11).

Is it possible that persons may have such an experience and then be disappointed with what they receive?

Sincere people, who truly love the Lord, have received this blessing with joy and ecstasy, but it was momentary and did not bring about the changes in their lives they had expected. For a few minutes they sensed the blessed nearness of the Lord, and from their inner being came strange words which they thought were praises to the Lord. But then they rationalized and decided it sounded like gibberish.

Suddenly it was over. They heard those who were praying with them say, "Praise the Lord! Another one has been baptized with the Holy Spirit, for we heard him speak in tongues."

Persons who had had such an unsatisfactory experience have left the Pentecostal prayer meeting and said, "There's

47

nothing to it. It's all just emotional excitement." Others may feel the same, but keep their feelings to themselves. In their hearts they too doubt the reality of the experience.

I know, for it was my experience.

I was told that, after I was baptized with the Spirit, I would have greater boldness in witnessing for Christ and greater power in prayer. I was also told the Bible would be easier to understand, for the Holy Spirit would illuminate the Word to my understanding.

It was explained to me that the Greek word for "power" is *dunamis,* the same word from which we get "dynamo" and "dynamite." When I received the Holy Spirit baptism, I was told, it would be like having a spiritual powerhouse within me. And I was taught that the initial evidence that I had received this experience was to speak in tongues, even if only a few words.

When a more mature brother in the Lord asked me if I had received the baptism in the Holy Spirit, I told him I didn't know. He sensed my confusion and, with patience and a knowledge of the Word, led me to an understanding of the experience I had received. He pointed out that although speaking in tongues is the initial sign one has received the Holy Spirit baptism, it is not the ultimate.

Even as the cry of a newborn baby is not the ultimate evidence of life, it may be considered the initial sign of life. But who would be pleased with a baby that gave no other evidence of life than an occasional cry? No one expects such a child to develop instantly into full stature and demonstrate the strength and wisdom and ability of an adult.

He explained that Jesus said, "And I will pray the Father, and he shall give you another Comforter, that he may abide with you forever, even the Spirit of truth; whom the world cannot receive, because it seeth him not, neither knoweth Him; but ye know him; for he dwelleth with you, and shall be in you" (John 14:16,17).

Jesus also said, "But the Comforter, which is the Holy Ghost, whom the Father will send in my name, he shall teach you all things, and bring all things to your remembrance, whatsoever I have said unto you" (John 14:26).

My friend showed me that the word "Comforter" means "helper," one who is called alongside to help carry the load.

He reminded me that some of the last words Jesus spoke to His disciples before His ascension were: "Ye shall be baptized with the Holy Ghost not many days hence ... ye shall receive power after that the Holy Ghost is come upon you" (Acts 1:5,8). Power to witness, power to pray, power to serve, power to overcome, power to control self, power to love, power to worship God in spirit and in truth.

I learned this would be experienced in the daily outworking of the Holy Spirit as I yielded to Him. I began to see that I was seeking for and wanting the experience of speaking in tongues so I'd be a part of the "in" crowd—rather than desiring and thirsting for the presence of the Spirit himself. I wanted the blessing rather than the Blesser; I sought the reward rather than the Rewarder; I desired the gift rather than the Giver.

So my friend encouraged me to seek the Lord and draw near to Him, to just express my love and appreciation for Him in the best way I knew.

When I got my spiritual priorities in order, I sought a closer walk with Him. And that night I received an experience that was not disappointing. Yes, I did speak in tongues, but this was merely incidental compared to the warmth of God's love that flooded my soul. In the Spirit I sensed I was seated in heavenly places with Him.

Praise and worship and expressions of love to my wonderful Lord became as spontaneous as breathing. Also the ministries Jesus said the Holy Spirit would perform in me have become a reality.

Disappointing Baptism? Not if we seek the Baptizer, rather than just an experience. The Baptism should not be merely a one-time experience but the beginning of a life in the Spirit.

Praise God; it is real; it is for everyone. All may "receive the gift of the Holy Ghost. For the promise is unto you, and to your children, and to all that are afar off, even as many as the Lord our God shall call" (Acts 2:38,39).

C.L. Strom, an Assemblies of God minister, lives in Springfield, Missouri.

10

WHAT ROLE SHOULD THE HOLY SPIRIT PLAY IN THE LOCAL CHURCH?

By Ralph M. Riggs

The Holy Spirit dwells in the church at large. He also dwells and operates in an ordained manner in each local church.

He draws the saints together

"By one Spirit are we all baptized into one body ... and have all been made to drink into one Spirit" (1 Corinthians 12:13). "Now ye are the body of Christ and members in particular" (v.27).

This intimate relationship makes Christians one with each other. Here is organism, as well as organization; unity, as well as union. This Spirit relationship draws us to each other as a magnet draws pieces of steel—"not forsaking the assembling of ourselves together" (Hebrews 10:25). We are together in the Holy Spirit.

He dictates the order of service

When the whole church comes together in one place, what is the scriptural procedure? "Exhort one another" (Hebrews 3:13). "Comfort one another" (1 Thessalonians 4:18). "Teaching and admonishing one another in psalms and hymns and spiritual songs" (Colossians 3:16). "Pray one for another" (James 5:16). "Love one another" (1 Peter 1:22). "Bear ye one another's burdens" (Galatians 6:2).

Congregational worship is at its purest when every member of the body is participating, when the whole body is animated, inspired and indwelt by the Holy Spirit and yielded to His operation.

He provides workers and operates through them

"God hath set some in the church" (1 Corinthians 12:28). He "gave gifts unto men. ... And he gave some, apostles; and some, prophets; and some, evangelists; and some, pastors and teachers; for the perfecting of the saints, for the work of the ministry, for the edifying of the body of Christ" (Ephesians 4:8,11,12).

These ministries should be active in the local church. Healings, tongues, and Spirit-led business meetings should occur and function in the power of the Holy Spirit.

He anoints the preaching

"For our gospel came not unto you in word only, but also in power, and in the Holy Ghost, and in much assurance" (1 Thessalonians 1:5). Peter speaks of preaching the gospel with the Holy Ghost sent down from heaven (1 Peter 1:12). Preaching with enticing words of man's wisdom, or with excellency of speech which is purely natural, is as much an intrusion of the profane into the holy as an admission of a Canaanite into the house of the Lord (Zechariah 14:21). Paul preached with the Holy Spirit gift of the word of wisdom and dared not preach otherwise (1 Corinthians 1,2).

He blesses the singing

"I will sing with the Spirit, and I will sing with the understanding also" (1 Corinthians 14:15). Here is Holy Spirit singing—the outflow of the Spirit-filled experience. It is "to the Lord," not to the audience. Let the praises of God be in our mouths. How better can we praise our God than with the Spirit of praise whom He has given us?

He directs the praying

Jude 20 says, "Praying in the Holy Ghost." The Holy Spirit stands ready to take control of yielded vessels and pray through them. No one knows better than He what we ought to pray for. As we yield our thoughts and our tongues, He will pray through us according to the will of God (Romans 8:26,27).

When Paul commands that we pray always with all prayer and supplication *in the Spirit*, he means praying *in the Spirit* (Ephesians 6:18). At this point the believer and the church face heavenward, acknowledge God as the Source of all blessing, thank Him for those blessings, bless Him, and minister unto Him. They that worship Him must "worship ... in spirit and in truth. The Father seeketh such to worship him" (John 4:23,24). How can we better worship Him than to worship in the Spirit, yielding our voices to His utterance? "For through him we both have access *by one Spirit* unto the Father" (Ephesians 2:18). In, by, and through the Holy Spirit, we should pray to the Father.

He influences our worship in many ways

Concerted praying. "They lifted up their voice to God with one accord and said, Lord, thou art God" (Acts 4:24). Since worship is personal and individual, all believers should be given individual opportunity to pour out their hearts to God in prayer. Why should the church have the stillness of a cemetery? This is the quietest world in which men will ever live. The wicked spend their eternity where there is weeping and gnashing of teeth and the shrieks and moans of the damned. The redeemed join the angels in praising God with a loud voice (Revelation 5:8-12). And the living creatures "rest not day and night, saying Holy, holy, holy, Lord God Almighty, which was, and is, and is to come" (Revelation 4:8).

Prophesying. "Despise not prophesyings" (1 Thessalonians 5:20); "Forbid not to speak with tongues" (1 Corinthians 14:39). Speaking forth under the unction of the Holy Spirit (as He gives utterance) in a known or unknown tongue by the rank-and-file members of the church is God-ordained and should occur in our churches. In Paul's time, these gifts were abused and exercised to excess; that is why the Thessalonians had quenched the Spirit, and why Paul spoke so much about the regulation of these gifts (1 Corinthians 14). The scriptural rule governing the operation of these gifts is that the prophets should speak one by one and not more than three in one service (v.29). They who have the gift of tongues should likewise speak not more than three messages in one service, and the tongues should be interpreted (v.27). Tongues plus interpretation equals prophecy. These rules are mandatory. "If any man think himself to be a prophet, or spiritual, let him acknowledge that the things that I write unto you are the commandments of the Lord" (1 Corinthians 14:37). Let none of us transgress or cause the full gospel to suffer by carelessness or disobedience in these matters.

Lifting up holy hands. "I will therefore that men pray everywhere, lifting up holy hands, without wrath and doubting" (1 Timothy 2:8). "Lift up your hands in the sanctuary and bless the Lord" (Psalm 134:2). Saints in prayer or praise lift up their hands and reach out to God. This beautiful expression of yearning and yielding to God should be welcomed.

Dancing in the Spirit. "Let them praise his name in the dance" (Psalm 149:3). "Praise him with the timbrel and dance" (Psalm 150:4). "David danced before the Lord with all his might" (2 Samuel 6:14). Michal, his wife, saw him and despised him in her heart; and upon his return home, she ridiculed him. David answered, "It was before the Lord

... therefore will I play before the Lord." God accepted David's method of praise and punished Michal (vv.16,21,23). Let modern Michals take note and beware.

Shouting. "Make a joyful noise unto the Lord, all the earth: make a loud noise, and rejoice, and sing praise" (Psalm 98:4). "Shout unto God with the voice of triumph" (Psalm 47:1). On Christ's triumphal entry into Jerusalem "the whole multitude of the disciples began to rejoice and praise God with a loud voice for all the mighty works that they had seen. ... And some of the Pharisees from among the multitude said unto him, Master, rebuke thy disciples. And he answered and said unto them, I tell you that, if these should hold their peace, the stones would immediately cry out" (Luke 19:37-40).

Which shall we be: the Pharisees, or those who worship God with a loud voice?

Prostration. When John saw his vision on the isle of Patmos, he fell at the Lord's feet as dead (Revelation 1:17). In heaven, too, they fall before Him in holy reverence (Revelation 4:10). It is a spontaneous and perfectly natural reaction to the glory of the Almighty God. Receiving the baptism in the Holy Spirit is an occasion when many fall prostrate under the power of God. Staid congregations still sing: "Oh, that with yonder sacred throng, we at His feet may fall; we'll join the everlasting song, and crown Him Lord of all." Why this pious expression and expectation, with no entry now into that experience which honors God and brings overwhelming glory to one's soul?

It is not scriptural to suppress these emotional impulses, if they are spontaneous and sincere and are felt by those whose lives are pure and godly. On the other hand, they who worship God in the Spirit should carefully observe the scriptural law governing all spiritual manifestations. They are given to profit withal (1 Corinthians 12:7). The gifts and operation of the Spirit are for the purpose of edifying the church (1 Corinthians 14:4,5,12,17,26). This is a good rule by which to judge all physical manifestations in the worship of Spirit-filled saints. Tongues, prophecy, wisdom, knowledge, faith, and great personal sacrifice are of no avail, if they are not motivated by love (1 Corinthians 13).

If the exercise of our gift or personal blessing does not edify the church and profit withal, love dictates that we remain silent and control our spirit and our blessing.

Ralph M. Riggs (1895-1971) was general superintendent of the Assemblies of God from 1953-59.

11

WHAT IS THE PURPOSE OF SPIRITUAL GIFTS?

By Randy Hurst

The Holy Spirit led our founders to form the Assemblies of God during the Pentecostal revival early in this century. Most of the reasons they gave for forming the Fellowship related to reaching the world with the gospel of Jesus Christ. Unlike many church bodies, whose missions focused on just certain parts of the world, our early leaders were compelled by the Spirit to obey our Lord's command to "go into all the world and preach the gospel" (Mark 16:15*).

The boldness of our forefathers' unreserved response to our Lord's command is astounding. How could such a small group of Christians even consider attempting the task of preaching the gospel in all the world? Because they were truly Pentecostal. They believed both Jesus' command to reach the whole world and also His promise that they would receive the Holy Spirit's power to do it (Acts 1:8).

From the birth of this Fellowship, we have depended on God to do supernatural works. An essential part of the Pentecostal movement in this century has been a fresh

---

*Scripture references in this chapter are from the New King James Version, except where noted.

emphasis on spiritual gifts. The manifestation of spiritual gifts is at the heart of God's working in and through His people.

Jesus said, "I will build My church" (Matthew 16:18). Our Lord did not just lay the foundation for the Church; He is still actively building it. He fulfilled His promise and sent the Holy Spirit to empower us. Jesus Christ is the Baptizer. In the hymn "A Mighty Fortress," Martin Luther expressed it well, "The Spirit and the gifts are ours, thro' Him."

The most extensive passage in the New Testament concerning spiritual gifts is 1 Corinthians 12-14. The apostle Paul was responding to the Corinthian church's emphasis on certain gifts (particularly tongues), while they neglected more essential gifts. Though he was dealing with a specific problem in a particular time and place, the truths he taught to help the Corinthian church apply in all times and places and provide insight for other issues concerning spiritual gifts.

Power of the Gifts

Paul mentions all three members of the Trinity working through spiritual gifts: "Now there are varieties of gifts, but the same Spirit. There are varieties of ministries, but the same Lord. And there are diversities of activities, but it is the same God who works all in all" (12:4-6). God calls us not merely to work for Him ... but to work with Him (Mark 16:20). He is working in and through us. It is God who empowers through the gifts.

In chapter 12, we find two powerful ways the gifts are manifested:

First, the power of the gifts is seen in their unity. Paul uses the human body as an example of the Church. The body is not merely an illustration of the Church; it is a divinely inspired representation of what God intends the Church to be. God designed both the physical human body and the spiritual body (the Church). A body can't function if its parts don't work together.

The Early Church was a living example of the power of spiritual unity. After the first Christians were filled with the Holy Spirit they "were of one heart and soul" (Acts 4:32).

Paul says God has so composed the body that "there should be no division in the body, but that its parts should have equal concern for each other. If one part suffers, every part suffers with it; if one part is honored, every part rejoices with it" (1 Corinthians 12:25,26, NIV).

Second, the power of the gifts is seen in their variety. God has a purpose for each of the gifts. The Corinthian church focused on a few gifts (especially tongues), and consequently the building up of the church suffered because they did not fully appreciate all the gifts God has given. The very nature of the church is that it is "not one member but many" (1 Corinthians 12:14). God knows what the church needs. Each part of the body and each spiritual gift has an important purpose. If we don't recognize the beauty and power in the variety God has provided, we might make two misjudgments. We might devalue our own place in the body (vv.15,16). Or we might devalue someone else's place in the body (v.21).

Placement of the Gifts

Twice in chapter 12 Paul emphasizes that spiritual gifts and ministries are in the Church by the will and action of God himself. Spiritual gifts are not imparted by the will and action of man. God acts through people, but by His own will. Paul mentions that a gift was within Timothy through the laying on of Paul's hands (2 Timothy 1:6), and also through prophecy with the laying on of hands by the presbytery (1 Timothy 4:14). But he clearly shows that God has placed each gift in the body "as He pleased" (1 Corinthians 12:18). He also shows in verse 28 that "God has appointed" the various ministries in the church.

We are to "earnestly desire" spiritual gifts (12:31; 14:1). But we are not to pursue them. Spiritual gifts are not rewards or achievements. They are gifts or graces that are undeserved and imparted by the will of God for the good of the whole church. We are to pursue love, but only to desire spiritual gifts (14:1). Spiritual gifts are not trophies of spirituality, but gifts God has placed in the church to work His purposes.

Perspective on the Gifts

Paul never intended chapter 13 to stand alone as a beautiful piece of prose about love. He didn't write it to be framed in flowers to hang by itself on a wall. Rather, it is the center of Paul's teaching concerning spiritual gifts to provide perspective. To understand this passage, we must remember what the Corinthian church was like. Their problem was not the spiritual gifts. The problem was their wrong attitude toward the gifts.

He begins the passage with two powerful arguments:

First, he is showing that as great as spiritual gifts are, love is even greater.

Second, he is showing that as wonderful as the gifts are, without love, the gifts become ineffective.

He is not in any way depreciating spiritual gifts. Before he begins his instruction concerning love, he says, "I show you a more excellent way" (12:31). The gifts are excellent. But love is "more excellent." Love is not in competition with the gifts. Love is what makes the gifts effective.

Purpose of the Gifts

The purpose of the gifts is to edify, which simply means to build up. It is related to the same word Paul uses in chapter 3 when he tells the Christians that we are God's building. Jesus is building His church. And He graciously uses us in His work.

He shows that the gifts build up in two ways. We are spiritually built up as individuals and the church is built up as a group (14:4).

Both are needed. The church is people. Individual people in the church need building up in order for the church as a whole to be built up.

Because it was a major issue in the Corinthian church, Paul uses tongues as an example. He makes a distinction between tongues that are interpreted in church gatherings and tongues that are only for personal edification. In church gatherings, tongues result in the building up of the church only if they are interpreted. Paul uses a very strong argument to show that when believers assemble together, the priority should be the building up of the whole church. To ensure the Corinthians do not think he is depreciating the value of tongues for personal edification, he says, "I thank my God I speak with tongues more than you all" (v.18). He goes on to say that in the church he would rather speak five words that are understood and instruct others than 10,000 in a language that is not understood (v.19). He is not devaluing tongues. He is establishing a priority.

At the close of the passage concerning spiritual gifts, to again make sure he is not misunderstood, he says, "Do not forbid to speak with tongues" (v.39). The priority is found in verse 12: "Let it be for the edification of the church that you seek to excel."

Propriety of the Gifts

God has chosen to manifest His gifts through people. But it is possible for people to misuse the gifts. Divinely directed order is needed for their proper use.

The purpose of the gifts (edification or building up) is the foundation for determining the propriety of the gifts. Paul says, "Let all things be done for edification" (v.26). He then gives practical teaching concerning the proper exercise of the gifts in church. Paul's last instruction concerning spiritual gifts is, "Let all things be done decently and in order" (v.40).

God does not control us as though we are puppets. We have a will. God's Spirit is working in us, but our own human spirit is still active and is subject to us (v.32). We can choose to control our spirit. The perspective of godly, selfless love in chapter 13 requires that each person submit to the common good of the rest of the church.

There is a proper time and place for each manifestation. God has not given us a complete list of exactly what is proper in each situation. What is proper and orderly in a prayer meeting might not be in a Sunday morning worship service. And what is in order at one time in a particular service might not be at another time in the same service. There is a time for personal edification and a time for edification of the whole church. God has given us leaders who are accountable to God to make those judgments.

God has appointed "administrations" in the church (v.28).

This word originally was used of steering a ship. It meant to govern by active guidance and direction. Leadership involves making judgments. When the leader of a service makes a decision concerning the propriety of a manifestation, that decision is under the guidance of the Spirit and is just as necessary as a message of prophecy or other gifts. And because the nature of "administrations" is "governing," the leader's judgment has authority over the exercise of the other gifts. The leader is accountable to God to be sensitive to what the Spirit wants to accomplish in a service and to be responsible that everything be proper and orderly.

Propriety in the use of the gifts is essential to their ongoing effectiveness because, tragically, misuse of spiritual gifts eventually results in disuse of the gifts. And the gifts are essential to the building of Christ's church. They are not merely intended for intermittent use, but as an ongoing means of empowering the Church to accomplish God's purposes. When Paul tells the Ephesian Christians to "be filled with the Spirit," the Greek verb he uses means to keep choosing to be filled (Ephesians 5:18). The infilling of the Spirit was not intended to be just an event. It should be a way of living.

A theme Scripture of our Fellowship appears on every cover of the *Pentecostal Evangel*: "Not by might, nor by power, but by My Spirit, saith the Lord" (Zechariah 4:6, KJV). When the angel of the Lord spoke these words to Zechariah, he was given a vision of seven lamps on a lampstand. The fuel for the lamps was not in a vessel but two living olive trees on either side of the lampstand, which provided a continual supply of oil.

The trees can be an illustration of God's unlimited living resources for building the Church. Among those means are spiritual gifts. We need to do what Paul exhorted the Corinthian church twice in this passage, "Earnestly desire spiritual gifts."

Randy Hurst is commissioner of evangelism for the Assemblies of God.

12

WHAT ARE THE FUNCTIONS OF SPEAKING IN TONGUES?

By R.L. Brandt

God graciously accommodated our human language deficiency by providing the wonderful gift of tongues. Speaking in tongues is a supernatural gift that goes beyond man's natural ability. It is essentially a communicative tool of the human spirit. Here are five functions of speaking in tongues:

Communication

Tongues enable a person's spirit to communicate directly with the Father of spirits. The earliest recorded instance was when the 120 in the Upper Room in Jerusalem were filled with the Holy Spirit: "They were all filled with the Holy Ghost, and began to speak with other tongues, as the Spirit gave them utterance" (Acts 2:4). When the Holy Spirit fully possesses one's spirit, that person speaks in tongues.

The 120 did not speak to each other in tongues, for they already had a common language. Also, they were not addressing the multitude when they spoke in tongues, for the crowd had not yet gathered. The question is, "Whom were they addressing?" The single reasonable conclusion is that they were speaking to God.

What was this strange new communication toward God? It was worship in the Spirit—worship by which they magnified God and spoke freely of "the wonderful works of God" (Acts 2:11).

Indication

Tongues is the means whereby persons can know with certainty they are filled with the Holy Spirit; and, at the same time, know that others have also been filled. "And they of the circumcision which believed were astonished ... because that on the Gentiles also was poured out the gift of the Holy Ghost. For they heard them speak with tongues" (Acts 10:45,46).

Edification

Edification is an extremely valuable function of tongues—edification for the individual who speaks with tongues and edification for the church when it occurs in the church, followed by interpretation.

Paul wrote, "He that speaketh in an unknown tongue edifieth himself" (1 Corinthians 14:4). And he also wrote, "Seek that ye may excel to the edifying of the church. Wherefore let him that speaketh in an unknown tongue pray that he may interpret" (1 Corinthians 14:12,13).

Prayer in tongues is an effective means for edification. Every child of God can profit immeasurably by it. Paul wrote, "For if I pray in an unknown tongue, my spirit prayeth. ... What is it then? I will pray with the spirit ... " (1 Corinthians 14:14,15). Then he added, "I thank my God, I speak with tongues more than ye all" (1 Corinthians 14:18).

The late missionary Mark Buntain, known for his efforts on behalf of India's outcasts, illustrates what Paul was speaking about. Tongues-speaking to him was a constant experience. To spend any time with him was to hear him quietly speaking in tongues. Little wonder he blessed and influenced so many.

Intercession

Paul wrote: "Likewise the Spirit also helpeth our infirmities: for we know not what we should pray for as we ought: but the Spirit itself maketh intercession for us with groanings which cannot be uttered" (Romans 8:26). There is intercession wrought by the Spirit which is beyond ordinary human expression. It is my personal persuasion that he has in mind intercession in other tongues.

Signification

The final function is the sign function: "Wherefore tongues are for a sign, not to them that believe, but to them that believe not" (1 Corinthians 14:22).

On the Day of Pentecost, the crowd outside the Upper Room cried, "And how hear we every man in our own tongue, wherein we were born?" (Acts 2:8). "We do hear them speak in our tongues the wonderful works of God. And they were all amazed, and were in doubt, saying one to another, What meaneth this?" (Acts 2:11,12). Tongues-speaking signified then and today that God is in the midst of His people.

George Bryan, a Native American, married Terry, a Caucasian. Before he and his wife married, she invited him to attend a meeting. As he sat there, a woman began speaking in a foreign language. He listened, utterly amazed, for she spoke in Castilian Spanish. He had specialized in languages, in particular Castilian Spanish. To hear an ordinary person speak the language dumbfounded him. When he learned she spoke it by the Holy Spirit, he was convinced and surrendered his life to Christ.

Yes, speaking in tongues is a wonderful gift of God. By it, we are assured we have been filled with the Spirit. By it, we are spiritually built up, and we contribute to the building up of the church. By it, we make effective intercession. And by it, unbelievers are directed to God.

R.L. Brandt is an executive presbyter of the Assemblies of God. He lives in Billings, Montana.

III.

THE
HOLY SPIRIT
IN THE
CHRISTIAN'S
LIFE

13

HOW PRACTICAL IS THE PENTECOSTAL LIFESTYLE?

By Charles T. Crabtree

I met a distinguished-looking gentleman in his mid-40s, who immediately began to impress upon me how educated he was. After a few minutes of a well-rehearsed oral résumé, I must confess I was impressed. He had several advanced degrees from an outstanding college and a prestigious university.

I mentioned our conversation to the pastor who informed me that the man was a professional student. "He has never held down a decent job," the pastor said. "His wife works day and night to support the family and pay his school bill."

While advanced degrees are laudable and often necessary, they are worthless if there is no application in real life. It would be interesting to ask the man's wife how impressed she is with her husband's education.

Sadly, many people wish to impress the world with their long association with and knowledge of a particular religion or denomination without an attending personal witness of how their stated religious views and associations make a difference in their lives. They are all profession and no practice. They have learned the concepts and ideas of a religion, but they have not learned a working faith; that is, an applied faith which is at work Monday through Saturday.

Pentecost came to this world as a gifting of God to His people for the express purpose of moving a religious faith out of the realm of thought to action, from promise to possession, from helplessness to supernatural power. But most of all, Pentecost is to reveal Jesus Christ as Savior and the source of a new, abundant, overflowing life that changes everything.

Some people today have trouble defining and intellectualizing Pentecost. They are desperately trying to explain the unexplainable and analyze supernatural life. They remind me of the scientists who proved beyond any doubt that a bee with its large body and small wings cannot fly. One problem: The bee stung their theory to death.

From the beginning, Pentecost was intended to be applied in reality, not in theory. In His wisdom, God took the baptism in the Holy Spirit out of the theoretical by giving the believer an undeniable physical evidence when the believer was filled. That evidence is speaking with other tongues.

When a person becomes hungry for the gift of the Holy Spirit, that person does not have to be in doubt or question whether he or she is filled. The fact is those who receive the gift of the Holy Spirit _will_ speak in tongues.

Someone says to me, "I have received the gift of the Holy Spirit, but I haven't spoken in tongues."

I say, "The promise of the Father without tongues is just that ... a promise. The promise without tongues is not a possession just as a promise of a gift is not the reality of the gift itself. I believe I will receive a gift, but I cannot apply the gift until I have taken possession."

The world is looking for applied Christianity. The answer

to that need is in a church empowered by the Holy Spirit in New Testament fullness. It is difficult to argue about the supernatural when the evidence is physically seen and heard.

Our forefathers came into Pentecost because they saw and heard applied Pentecost. Thousands came out of dead, cold, analytical religion because they saw the mighty works of God in miracles of healing. Others came into Pentecost because they heard anointed preaching and singing. There was a dimension of God's presence and power beyond human ritual and form. Still others came into Pentecost because they heard about the fullness of the Spirit and then saw the results of that fullness in transformed lives.

Pentecost is the undeniable witness of a living Christ through human instrumentality. Pentecost is more than a doctrine to be questioned and analyzed; it is a reality to be sought after and possessed. Pentecost is proof positive that the gates of hell will not prevail against the church that believes the promises of God are applicable to the realities of life.

Charles T. Crabtree is assistant general superintendent of the Assemblies of God.

14

HOW CAN A PERSON HEAR THE VOICE OF THE SPIRIT?

By J.W. Jepson

The shadow of the truck and trailer stretched longer and longer as it cruised down Interstate 5. Cal* was a good driver with a clean record. This was his regular run, and he was familiar with this gray ribbon of highway.

The hum of the diesel droned in his ears, and his eyes scanned the road ahead. But Cal's thoughts were on something else. Deep inside a struggle raged. The pastor had been trying to turn him to Christ, and for weeks Cal had been under conviction of sin.

Suddenly something happened ahead. Cal had to take quick action, almost piling up his rig. Shaken by the experience, he went the next day to see the pastor. "Pastor," he said, his voice trembling with emotion, "I think God is telling me to get saved."

"I think so too," the pastor replied.

*Name has been changed.

Coincidence? Perhaps, but nothing like that had happened to Cal before. It occurred while the Holy Spirit was wrestling with his soul. The correlation was significant.

Yes, the Holy Spirit is talking to people. No, it is not usually in an audible voice, but He is communicating.

Nicodemus came to Jesus one night. Like the truck driver, his mind was on spiritual matters. Jesus told him, "Most assuredly, I say to you, unless one is born of water and the Spirit, he cannot enter the kingdom of God. ... The wind blows where it wishes, and you hear the sound of it, but cannot tell where it comes from and where it goes. So is everyone who is born of the Spirit" (John 3:5-8*).

We do not see the wind, but we witness the effects of its power. We do not see the Holy Spirit, but we observe the results of His influences on the human spirit. He urges the sinner to repent, trust Christ, and live for God. The heart yields, and the person is changed—born of the Spirit.

The Bible is the Holy Spirit's message, and He works diligently to call our attention to it. "So, as the Holy Spirit says: 'Today, if you hear his voice, do not harden your hearts' " (Hebrews 3:7,8, NIV). As He did the truck driver, He brings people into circumstances that reinforce the impression of truth upon the mind. He sharpens the conscience. He reproves the world of sin (John 16:8).

The Holy Spirit does not move the human will by force. His influence is moral, persuasive. He seeks to turn the heart by truth. He combines infinite values, eternal consideration, and powerful motives, and thrusts the full weight of their logic on the reason in a mighty effort to turn the soul to God.

But moral, persuasive influences can be accepted or rejected. You see a man standing on a high ledge about to jump. You have no way to restrain him physically. You have only one tool—persuasion. So you address his reason, urging the strongest, highest values and considerations you can muster. You appeal to his emotions with tender passion. But what he does with your plea is up to him. The

*Scripture references in this chapter are from the New King James Version, except where noted.

decision is his alone.

Sin is spiritual suicide. The Holy Spirit appeals to the reason, urging the strongest, highest values and considerations. Truth floods the sinner's mind, but what the soul does with the Spirit's gracious influences is its own choice.

The Holy Spirit is giving himself to the thankless task of winning people from self-destruction. But so long as they hold to their self-indulgences, they frustrate Him and make their own salvation impossible. No one can be born of the Spirit until he stops resisting the Spirit.

Acts 7 records Stephen's defense before the council. As he addressed them, he leveled this charge: "You always resist the Holy Spirit" (v.51).

These were religious men. They attended worship, tithed, prayed, fasted, read the Scriptures. Their public conduct was highly acceptable. Yet they always resisted the Holy Spirit. Not just often—always—while praying, fasting, tithing, attending worship. Because their hearts were wrong, everything was wrong. They did everything to be seen of men (Matthew 23:5).

The Holy Spirit wrestles with people because they stubbornly refuse to repent and believe the gospel.

How do people resist the Holy Spirit? By resisting the truth as He presents it to the mind. This is done by rejecting the truth outright, putting off obedience, diverting one's attention to something else, embracing error—by any action other than honest, immediate surrender to God.

It is alarming to see how willingly some professed Christians sin against the light. When they make up their minds to do what they want to do, what the Bible says no longer matters to them. "He who has an ear, let him hear what the Spirit says to the churches" (Revelation 2:7, NIV).

What does resisting the Holy Spirit lead to? What are its consequences? Jesus said, "If therefore the light that is in you is darkness, how great is that darkness!" (Matthew 6:23).

As the Holy Spirit is grieved (Ephesians 4:30), the heart becomes hard and cold. Truth no longer affects the soul. There is less and less interest in the gospel. The heart is unaffected by its presentation. The mind becomes settled in error and self-delusion.

The Bible records the tragedy of some who were successful in resisting the Holy Spirit. "But the Spirit of the Lord departed from Saul" (1 Samuel 16:14). Israel "rebelled and grieved His Holy Spirit; So He turned Himself against them as an enemy" (Isaiah 63:10).

Look at that precious soul. All heaven is filled with anxiety over him, and yet he trifles. Against the opposition of the Holy Spirit and his own reason, he stubbornly rejects the Savior. He dashes recklessly on, crashing every roadblock the Spirit of God throws in his path. Once the siren of conscience shattered his complacency as he raced down the broad way to destruction, but now it is almost silent.

There he is on the precipice. The Holy Spirit makes one last desperate effort to save him, but he wrenches himself from the Spirit's restraining grasp and plunges himself into everlasting torment. The sight is unbearable. Heaven groans in grief.

Proverbs 29:1 (NIV) warns, "A man who remains stiff-necked after many rebukes will suddenly be destroyed—without remedy."

God's Spirit is patiently telephoning people's hearts. They must answer while He is still calling.

J.W. Jepson, D.Min., is pastor of Life in Christ Center (Assemblies of God), The Dalles, Oregon.

15

HOW DOES THE SPIRIT GUIDE OUR LIVES?

By G. Raymond Carlson

L ife is filled with difficulties. But Christ has given us a
Helper to take the place of His visible presence. He said,
"I will pray the Father, to give you another Helper to be
with you forever" (John 14:16, Moffatt).

Two things are plain. First, I need divine help to live the
life that pleases God. Second, I can have all the help I need.

The first is demonstrated in experience. Someone said, "A
person needs to be made of steel to survive these days." But
who has that quality? We all need God's help.

The second is the promise made by Jesus. We can have all
the help we need. More than that, we can have the Helper
himself. How does He help? Paul wrote, "The Spirit ...
helpeth our infirmities" (Romans 8:26).

A Spiritual Airlift

Following World War II, the Soviets, as part of their cold
war strategy, cut off all food and fuel going into West Berlin,
which was occupied by the United States, Great Britain, and
France. Their objective: to starve and freeze the Berliners into

submission and to cause the Allies to withdraw. Roads to the city were closed, and the cause of the West looked bleak.

But the ingenuity and courage of the Allies hadn't been reckoned with. The Berlin Airlift brought supplies from the skies hour after hour, day after day, until the blockade was lifted. The Berliners did not starve, nor did they freeze. Neither did they surrender.

Sometimes we, like the Berliners, find ourselves hopelessly surrounded. Defeat seems certain. But then the Helper establishes His spiritual airlift and brings His limitless supply of whatever we need.

More Than a Coincidence

The Holy Spirit's ministries are varied. None of them should be ignored or neglected. One ministry is that of leading.

I was about to introduce the evening speaker. While I was still seated, the Spirit spoke to me, not audibly, but still in a real way: "You're going to have a funeral, and you're to use John 11:25 as your text." The impression was strong and kept repeating itself.

I knew of no one in my pastoral responsibility who was ill. But at that moment I noticed a woman step into the sanctuary. She spoke briefly to my wife who was seated at the back. Shortly my wife beckoned to me; and, after I presented the speaker, I slipped out a side door to get the message.

The woman requested I come immediately to a rest home to see her aged father who was extremely ill. I went and had the joy of leading him to the Savior. I returned to the service before the sermon concluded.

The next morning the woman told us her father had died minutes after I left. Then she said, "I'd like you to conduct the funeral. I know I shouldn't tell you what to take as a text, but could you use, 'I am the resurrection, and the life: he that believeth in me, though he were dead, yet shall he live'?"

That's John 11:25. It was my first funeral service and I was thankful for this experience. It was more than a coincidence; it was a leading by the Holy Spirit.

Prompted by the Spirit

God has chosen to lead His people by His Word and by His Spirit. (See Romans 8:14; Galatians 5:18.) Today when so much stress is placed upon guidance and counseling vocationally, educationally, and mentally, many children of God fail to avail themselves of the unerring guidance of the Spirit.

The Holy Spirit uses the Bible, the written, revealed will of God. His promptings will never violate the Scriptures, for He is the Author. (See 2 Peter 1:21.) But it is important to heed His promptings.

One day such a prompting came. Seemingly a hundred things were pressing upon me demanding attention. I became impressed to drop it all and make a trip to a neighboring state to call on some friends. The husband was not a Christian. We had a warm friendship, but he was opposed to the Pentecostal message. Arriving at their home, my wife and I were welcomed by the husband. "How good to see you," he said. "We desperately need help. Marie is very ill. Come in." We went into the bedroom, and the three of us— the unsaved husband, my wife and I—prayed by his wife's bed. God touched her. The husband was so moved he yielded himself to Christ. Today he is in heaven with the Savior he had turned aside for almost 80 years.

Higher Level of Knowledge

The Holy Spirit is more than a last resort to be used in case of emergency. He dwells in your heart, always remaining in the background, never speaking of himself. (See John 16:13.) He performs secret service on your behalf, efficiently and lovingly.

He seeks to be a gracious, willing Guest. Your job is to cultivate intimacy with Him. Listen to His promptings, pleadings, and wooings. Consult Him. Above all, openly accept the gifts of grace and enduement which He offers.

Before going to Calvary, Jesus said: "I have yet many things to say unto you, but ... the Spirit of truth ... will guide you into all truth ... show you things to come ... shall glorify me … shall receive of mine, and shall show it unto you" (John 16:12-15).

The Holy Spirit is the divine Teacher. He alone can discern and impart spiritual truth, for He is the Spirit of Truth. There is a stratum of knowledge to be gained in the material-physical realm, but there is a higher level of knowledge that can only be imparted by the Spirit. (See 1 Corinthians 2:1-13.)

This knowledge is not attained through education. Someone said, "You can pile up your training and add your degrees until finally you may totter with a cane across the last academic platform of your life, but that doesn't necessarily assure you of spiritual knowledge." Certain knowledge comes only through the ministry of the Spirit, through God's Word. Such knowledge comes not through just knowing about a Person, but through knowing Him. (See Philippians 3:10.)

The Holy Spirit reveals the things of God (1 Corinthians 2:10-13) and the things of Christ. (See John 16:14.) He gives insight concerning the future. (See Luke 2:26; John 16:13.) He helps recall the words of Christ (John 14:26) and provides answers for persecuted believers. (See Mark 13:11; Luke 12:12.) The Spirit guides into all truth. (See John 14:17; 16:13.) He provides the word of wisdom or the word of knowledge as needed (1 Corinthians 12:8) and guides the decisions of the Church. (See Acts 15:28.) He leads in the way of godliness. (See Isaiah 30:21; Ezekiel 36:27.)

Jesus said it was expedient for us that He return to heaven so He might send the Holy Spirit upon us. (See John 16:7.) Similarly it is expedient that we receive the Spirit, recognize His presence, and let Him do His work. Let us make much of the ministries of the Spirit of God to us, in us, and through us.

G. Raymond Carlson (1918-99) served as general superintendent of the Assemblies of God from 1986-93.

16

HOW CAN A RELATIONSHIP WITH THE HOLY SPIRIT BE NURTURED?

By George O. Wood

Scottish playwright James Barrie dolefully commented on the difference between our expectations for life and the realities we actually experience: "The life of every man is a diary in which he means to write one story, but instead writes another. And his saddest hour is when he compares the volume as it is with what he vowed to make it."

Such a statement reflects an attitude of disillusionment far from the promise of Jesus: "I have come that they may have life, and have it to the full" (John 10:10, NIV).

How can we be sure the end result of our living parallels the statement of Jesus rather than that of James Barrie?

The Bible has clear answers.

Most of the time our concern for life has to do with living better here and now. But God has a more expansive view. He seeks to empower us to live eternally.

No matter how much money, power, health, or success you have, it will not exempt you from dying. Only Jesus can give you resurrection-order life—whether you are wealthy or on welfare; whether you have great influence or none—regardless of age, gender, or ethnicity. Life is not available outside of Jesus Christ.

So begin with Him. Confess your sin and need to Him (1 John 1:9). Ask Him to enter your life (Revelation 3:20). Believe on Him with your heart and confess Him as Lord with your mouth (Romans 10:8,9). Follow Him by being baptized in water and learning His way of life and thinking (Matthew 28:19). Commit yourself to be part of His church (Acts 2:42).

The Lord has a wonderful gift for you along with salvation: the baptism in the Holy Spirit (Acts 1:8; 2:4,38,39). You cannot live the Christian life under your own power, nor can you effectively witness to others about your newfound faith unless the Spirit of God enables you. The purpose of the baptism in the Holy Spirit is to so overwhelm you with the presence of God that you will no longer dwell on your own weaknesses and inadequacies, but instead be filled with assurance and boldness.

Have you noticed how two persons accomplish the same job? Look at the difference between the 15th and 16th presidents of the United States. Immediately we recognize the 16th president as Abraham Lincoln, but are hard pressed to recall the name of the 15th. Why? Both held the same office and faced the crisis of a nation divided over the issue of slavery. What made the difference? One, Lincoln, had a personal enablement; the other didn't. It wasn't their constitutional powers which made the difference. Both exercised identical legal authority as president. It was a personal empowerment in Lincoln not possessed by the 15th president.

It is equally possible for us to live our Christian life as that unremembered 15th president.

We have the office of being a Christian, but are devoid of the power. That is why we need the baptism in the Spirit and the ongoing filling of the Spirit to bring a song to our hearts, thanksgiving to our lips, and proper relationships with others (Ephesians 5:18-21).

Have you given your life to the Lord? Have you received the baptism in the Holy Spirit?

Are you continually full of the Spirit's presence? If the answer to any of these questions is no, then ask the Lord to meet you at the level of the need you have right now. Seek a pastor or mature Christian to pray and counsel with you.

What comes after conversion, water baptism, the baptism in the Spirit, linkage and identification with the local church? How do we live empowered each day with strength to overcome the sadness and hurt of life, and invigoration to challenge the monotony and humdrum of daily existence?

Here's a checklist for daily use:

1. *Have I opened the Bible today and let it speak to me?*

Failing to take God's Word into your life is like neglecting to eat. You become weak when you do not receive nourishment.

2. *Have I prayed meaningfully today?*

I use my hand as a prayer guide: the thumb represents persons who are nearest my heart; the index finger, those who are an example and point the way; the middle finger, those who are in places of temporal and spiritual authority; the next finger, my weakest, those in great need and vulnerability; and the little finger, me—the smallest and least.

3. *Is there sin, bitterness, or unforgiveness in my life?*

I need to practice daily spiritual cleansing and not let impurity build up and become caked into my life. Each night as I go to sleep I must seek to do so with a clear conscience (Ephesians 4:26).

4. *Am I sensitive to how God may want to guide or use me today?*

Peter prayed during the noon hour, and the Lord changed the destiny of Cornelius and his family because Peter opened himself to being guided of the Lord (Acts 10:9). I must not live so structured that I block out what God may want me to do. And when I know what He wants, I must obey.

5. *Have I sought to help or encourage someone today whose need is greater than my own?*

The Lord commended to us the example of the Good Samaritan (Luke 10:30-37). When I am emotionally expended or dealing with personal hurt and sorrow, I must rise above my concerns to enter in to the concerns of another. The Lord is my example. On His cross He focused on the needs of others for forgiveness, pardon, and support.

6. *Do I live, as Jesus taught, one day at a time (Matthew 6:11,25-34)?*

I cannot be empowered to live the future unless I am empowered to live today. I must not daydream about how different today would be if I could order it so. God has given me today and seeks for me to glorify Him in it. If I am faithful in small responsibilities now, He will decide what my lot will be tomorrow.

7. *Have I relinquished myself to His full control this day?*

Sometimes hurtful things hit us and we feel diminished. How can we live to the full when we have taken a hard blow to the midsection and the air has been knocked out of us? We must change our focus from asking why to asking what now.

In Romans 8 Paul did not concentrate on the why, but the what. In so doing he reminded us that the future glory will be greater than any present suffering. The Holy Spirit is interceding for us even when we don't have words because the pain is too great; God is always working for the good; nothing can separate us from the Lord. In such times I am empowered as I realize how much God loves me, guards me, and cares for me. He has a stronger grip on me than I have on Him.

Out of this daily relationship with the Lord flows the quality of life in which we are empowered to be persons of love, joy, peace, patience, kindness, goodness, faithfulness, gentleness, and self-control (Galatians 5:22,23).

The other day I flew in a private plane. I took the co-pilot's seat even though I don't know how to fly a plane. I noticed that each time the pilot pulled on the stick, the identical stick for the co-pilot's seat mimically moved in the same direction. The needles on my duplicate side of the instrument panel registered the same as those on his side.

Empowerment to live as a Christian is like flying in that

co-pilot's seat. As long as I don't take the stick or the throttle, but let Him do the piloting, it's a good and safe trip. It would be absurd for me to attempt to take controls from Him when He is on the plane. I must let Him move the controls and monitor the gauges. When the day comes that I know enough about flying, then He can monitor my progress; and if I fly the plane like He would, He will let me continue. But no matter how experienced I may become, I must always yield control to Him.

If I want to live empowered, then each day I will sit in my co-pilot's seat, go through the checklist He asks of me, but make sure that I never attempt to fly the plane by myself or without His direction and approval. My empowerment comes from Him. So must yours.

By the way ... in case you wondered ... the name of our 15th president was James Buchanan.

George O. Wood, D.Th.P., is general secretary of the Assemblies of God.

17

HOW DOES THE SPIRIT HELP US SERVE?

By T. Ray Rachels

The most famous address for modern-day Pentecostals is 312 Azusa Street in Los Angeles. There in 1906 God sent the Holy Spirit to awaken the church with a revival that lasted three years.

City officials took down the street sign several years ago because it's only an alleyway, a half-block long, adjacent to the Japanese Cultural Center. They assumed it didn't merit identification.

A few concerned Pentecostal citizens appealed to Mayor Tom Bradley to restore the sign. "It's a historic site," they said. "Something significant happened there, and it must not be forgotten."

The sign is up again. Azusa Street has its name back. Just a little street. Why notice?

From Azusa Street and the revival of 1906, more than 523 million people today are Pentecostal Christians, according to *The World Christian Encyclopedia* (2000 edition). All trace their roots to what happened at that place—the baptism in the Holy Spirit with the initial physical evidence of speaking in other tongues. The result was spiritual backbone; fearless witness; willingness to suffer; an overwhelming love, joy, and enthusiasm; a missionary spirit.

The resources from God's hand were so unexpected that they caught everyone off guard. The church suddenly was empowered in ways she had long forgotten.

The task for us is to properly interpret the Spirit of Pentecost for today. What does the Spirit say to you and me? Surely His coming was to point us to God and His glory.

Here are three principles that today's believers can embrace:

God's glory is revealed to people who follow Jesus

This challenge was once posed to evangelist Dwight L. Moody: "The world has yet to see what God will do with a man fully consecrated to Him." Moody determined to be that man.

The great need of the church is for people of the Spirit who are totally committed to Christ. Without the Spirit no amount of intellectual power, administrative ability or even the capacity to work without fatigue will bring us through. It is "by my Spirit, saith the Lord" (Zechariah 4:6*).

People who follow Jesus are called to serve as He served

Jesus revealed a revolutionary idea of greatness at the Last Supper. "He rose from supper, laid aside His garments, and girded himself with a towel ... and began to wash the disciples' feet" (John 13:4,5).

Greatness in the kingdom of God is measured in terms of service.

Michael Green in his book, *Called To Serve*, said that Peter learned his lesson well, because in his epistle he used the word "submit" again and again. It is applied to husbands and wives, young and old, slaves and leaders.

Peter also said, "Clothe yourselves, all of you with humility" (1 Peter 5:5). The likely meaning intended, according to Green, is that we are to do our service for God in a way simi-

*Scripture references in this chapter are from the Revised Standard Version, except where noted.

lar to that of Jesus when He took a towel and girded himself. It's Peter's way of saying that believers are to have this characteristic of Jesus. A believer who does not bear the mark of humble servanthood does not reflect the glory of God.

Paul wrote, "You are not your own; you were bought at a price" (1 Corinthians 6:19,20, NIV). His reference was to the Roman slave and his master. The slave had no rights. His money, time, future, and marriage were at the disposal of his master.

New Testament writers delighted to call themselves slaves of Christ. It was their description of a Christian. Status had an unholy ring to it, for they had all things in common.

"Paul, a servant [slave] of Jesus Christ, called to be an apostle, set apart for the gospel of God" (Romans 1:1).

"But now that you have been set free from sin and have become slaves of God, the return you get is sanctification and its end, eternal life" (Romans 6:22). (See also Philippians 1:1; Titus 1:1; James 1:1; 2 Peter 1:1; and Jude 1.)

"When we reflect on the history of the church," wrote Green, "are we not bound to confess that she has failed to follow the example of her Founder? All too often she has worn the robes of the ruler, not the apron of the servant."

People who serve as Christ served will be empowered by the Spirit who comes to reveal the glory of God

To whom can we look today for renewal? The Holy Spirit offers himself.

In Greek mythology one labor of Hercules was to clean the stables of Augeas. In them Augeas had stabled 3,000 head of oxen for 30 years without ever once cleaning them. It was Hercules' task to clear away this accumulation of filth. He did not even attempt to do it himself. The myth says he deflected the course of two rivers so they flowed through the stables, and their cleansing tide did what no human effort could have done.

The Holy Spirit links a man with a power far greater than his own, says William Barclay, Scottish biblical scholar, and that flood tide of cleansing and renewing does for him what he himself could never do.

Bezaleel was picked out for mention in Exodus. "The Lord … has filled him with the Spirit of God, with ability, with intelligence, with knowledge, and with all craftsmanship, to devise artistic designs, to work in gold and silver and bronze, in cutting stones for setting, and in carving wood, for work in every skilled craft. And he has inspired him to teach" (Exodus 35:30-34).

This moves theology into the workplace. The Spirit of God stands squarely in the center of daily routine, in the mechanic's shop, on the carpenter's table, on the assembly line, at the secretary's desk, and on the salesman's route. God intends to be in the middle of your life's work, and His Spirit is promised to you for help.

Whatever gift a man has—of mind, heart, brain, eye, or hand—is the gift of the Spirit. It is not only the preacher in his study or pulpit who is working in the power of the Spirit; the man or woman whose work is dedicated to God and His glory, however lofty or humble, is also working in the power of the Spirit.

I saw this gift eloquently demonstrated in a large church gathering. The Word of God had been delivered. People were praying. God was moving in rich power.

Then, the pianist played—softly at first, holding her music underneath the 2,000 praying people. Then she began playing boldly, beautifully, majestically, with authority, singing the songs as she played.

Her music and presence grew into a dominant theme. No person interrupted. The gift of God was at work.

The attention of my spirit, and others as well, riveted on such joyous abandonment. With her eyes closed, lost in wonder, there was divine transport in her contribution to the Holy Spirit's movement of grace. God's glory was upon her and upon us as well. She had taken what she had, lifted it to God, and God had distributed it among the people.

Regardless of how great or small our abilities are, with the empowering of the Holy Spirit they are enough to accomplish His purposes.

T. Ray Rachels is superintendent of the Southern California District of the Assemblies of God.

18

HOW DOES THE SPIRIT ASSIST IN WITNESSING?

By C.M. Ward

The Holy Spirit must fit the believer for the task of soul winning. The Holy Spirit must also prepare the one receiving the witness and provide the opportunity.

I cannot *convict*. He can. I cannot *empower* to believe. He can. I cannot *enlighten*. He can. I cannot *assure*. He can. The Acts of the Apostles is the text that proves it.

There are 14 reasons set forth in this New Testament book.

1. *The Holy Spirit bestows power*. I dare not, unless I am most foolish, enter battle otherwise.

My intent as a believer is to capture a member among the enemy. This means conflict. Every resource of darkness will be marshaled against me.

God affords me strength only in the Holy Spirit. My strength is never in myself lest I be tempted to use such strength wrongfully. "Ye shall receive power, when the Holy Spirit is come upon you" (Acts 1:8, ASV).

2. *The Holy Spirit gives utterance*. No substitute is ever equal. What the Holy Spirit provides in anointed speech is beyond any lesson in public speaking or any adequacy gained by education.

The best of us need "utterance." There is a compulsion that convinces the hearer that God is at work. The utterance fits the occasion.

3. *The Holy Spirit inspires boldness.* There are two drags on me which repeatedly hinder my witness. There is the timidity of the flesh and the boldness of the flesh. I can lag. I can presume. There are times when I need to be quiet and allow the Spirit to work.

I have discovered this in giving the altar invitation. Often I talk too much. Other times I speak and give offense when what is needed is tenderness.

The boldness of the Spirit is a rare combination of the courage of the lion and the gentleness of the dove.

4. *The Holy Spirit requires purity.* The witness of Ananias and Sapphira was repudiated. The Holy Spirit is a zealous and jealous Protector of Calvary's message. The Holy Spirit exercises stern discipline. He will not lower the standards of heaven. The Holy Spirit does not allow the sinner to be mis-led by false claims.

5. *The Holy Spirit cooperates with the witness.* "We are his witnesses ... and so is also the Holy Ghost" (Acts 5:32). Peter made that statement to the Sanhedrin. They had challenged his right to preach. They claimed he was unauthorized. Peter had a backing they neither controlled nor understood. That leads to confidence, and confidence is rewarded.

Here is a word of caution. The Holy Spirit is not at our beck and call to support what we do on our own initiative. We must obey His leading. Then we have His support. Until we learn this lesson, we experience frustration.

6. *The Holy Spirit directs organization.* God requires a vehicle. It is difficult to obtain proper results from improper means. You can't win the Kentucky Derby with a mule.

One of the first lessons in Acts is the need of reorganiza-tion. The apostles were at the wrong end of things. As a result, the spread of the gospel was hindered. The Holy Spirit revealed the correction. It worked.

Everywhere there are spiritual defects in organization and presentation. It isn't a matter of bad people. It is a matter of good people making bad mistakes.

Personal lives need to be organized by the Holy Spirit. Many Christians are lacking in usefulness because of a lack of order. Lives are cluttered. Investments are wasted. These need what recruits need. They need discipline and direction. Results would be forthcoming. So many of us are our own worst enemies.

A strange heresy persists. It is that the freedom of the Spirit and lack of organization are synonymous. All God's works reveal Him as a God of order, budget, and schedule. The Spirit-directed life will reflect this attribute of God.

7. *The Holy Spirit orders expansion*. The perimeter is always enlarging. Growth is a vital sign. Never permit anyone to convince you otherwise. The temptation of the flesh is toward comfortable consolidation.

The Holy Spirit stirred the nest at Jerusalem and resorted to drastic means—persecution. The witness was scattered. Pressure forced expansion.

8. *The Holy Spirit breaks down barriers*. The Holy Spirit can integrate faster than any civil legislation can. He doesn't recognize the distinctions that human beings love to catalog. Jesus didn't ask permission to speak to the Samaritan lady.

Philip, the evangelist, didn't ask tradition for permission before riding with and talking to the Ethiopian.

Peter had to abandon his kosher prejudice and preach to the household of Cornelius.

Once again the Holy Spirit is moving among us to attack prejudice and cross lines. Time builds custom and alibis and a lot of synthetic thinking. Only the Holy Spirit can pull down these "vain imaginations." Thank God He is doing it in a remarkable demonstration of charismatic renewal. Spirit-filled people delight in newfound freedoms.

9. *The Holy Spirit overcomes satanic power*. That antagonism is often expressed through men, but they are not our foe. Satan, behind them, is the real enemy, for "we wrestle not against flesh and blood" (Ephesians 6:12). Too often, tragically, we find ourselves wrestling in the flesh and without the Holy Spirit present. The result hinders the spread of

the gospel. Spats and snipings never advance the gospel.

When facing satanic power, I have learned to say, "The Lord rebuke you!" No believer, in himself or herself, is adequate to close in with Satan. The Holy Spirit can and will. His authority is adequate.

10. *The Holy Spirit directs the witness*. Not every direction is God's direction. Paul learned that God's choice did not coincide with his choice, although Paul felt his decision was a good one. He wanted to go east, but God commanded him to go west. Obedience is an ingredient of success. It was for Paul.

The Holy Spirit will faithfully provide the burden. In this case Paul saw in a vision the man of Macedonia and an appeal for help. Effective witnessing is witnessing which is directed by the Holy Spirit, not by natural urges. It means curbing the human impulse and recognizing the leading of the Spirit.

11. *The Holy Spirit prepares hearts*. It is said that Lydia, the Thessalonian, was one "whose heart the Lord opened" (Acts 16:14).

If God doesn't open the heart, nothing I can ever say or do will open it. It can never be my persuasion, my tact, my repertoire. It must be the work of the Holy Spirit. It's so simple but true: Revival depends on the Holy Spirit rather than on methods.

12. *The Holy Spirit enlightens believers*. Assurance is a big part of it. I must know that I have passed from death to life. This knowledge is the work of the Spirit. This is faith that quickens—that is alive—circulating in the believer. It is beyond head knowledge; it is heart knowledge.

There were disciples in Ephesus who "knowing only the baptism of John" (Acts 18:25) needed much more. They were groping. They were victims of imperfect instruction. They needed help. The Holy Spirit provided it for them.

13. *The Holy Spirit confounds mimicry*. There will always be imitations. Where there is healing, deliverance, joy, and success, there will always be attempts to preempt such a market. The temptation to reap financial gain is strong. So the unworthy may venture to use that "name which is above

every name" (Philippians 2:9). They wish to magnify themselves. The Holy Spirit dclineates such attempts.

14. *The Holy Spirit gives discernment*. He makes the servant of God master of the situation. You are given eyes of another world to see what a world system cannot see. It is the believer's advantage. Paul saw amid the Mediterranean storm what captain, crew, and passengers could not see. Holy Spirit discernment made him the man of the hour.

The Holy Spirit immediately directs us toward those steps by which men and women may be saved.

That is why I say with all the power of my soul that it is "not by might, nor by power, but by my Spirit, saith the Lord of hosts" (Zechariah 4:6). We are absolutely dependent upon the Holy Spirit.

C.M. Ward (1909-96) was *Revivaltime* broadcast speaker for 25 years.

19

WHAT IS PRAYING IN THE SPIRIT?

By Hardy W. Steinberg

J esus had finished praying, and the disciples asked, "Lord, teach us to pray" (Luke 11:1). Today we still profit from the guidance He gave in what is commonly referred to as the Lord's Prayer.

Now the Holy Spirit, another Comforter just like Jesus, is with us (John 14:16,17). Jesus said He will teach us all things (John 14:26). Since He inspired writers of Scripture to instruct believers to pray in the Spirit, He will also teach us how if we want to learn.

Nature of Prayer in the Spirit

The Bible indicates that not all prayer is effective. James said those who waver in faith, who look in two directions, would not receive anything from the Lord (James 1:7). To those who pray while regarding iniquity in their hearts, the Psalmist said, "The Lord will not hear" (Psalm 66:18). To those who pray to be seen of men, Jesus said they have their reward in the attention they receive (Matthew 6:5). Those who pray for things because of carnal desires will not receive what they ask for (James 4:3).

But the Bible also talks about effective prayer, about praying in the Spirit. Paul wrote, "Praying always with all prayer and supplication in the Spirit, and watching thereunto with all perseverance and supplication for all saints" (Ephesians 6:18). Jude wrote, "But ye, beloved, building up yourselves on your most holy faith, praying in the Holy Ghost" (Jude 20). This is effective prayer, so God's people need to learn what they can about it.

Praying in the Spirit is prayer that is directed by the Spirit. Sometimes this guidance comes from the Word of God. Daniel's prayer of confession and intercession for the Jews' return to Jerusalem came after reading Jeremiah's prophecy concerning 70 years of divine chastening (Daniel 9:1-3). People who have learned to pray in the Spirit are people who spend time with God's Word and are governed by it.

Sometimes direction for prayer comes from a report. When Nehemiah heard of the deplorable conditions in Jerusalem, he wrote, "When I heard these words ... I sat down and wept, and mourned certain days, and fasted, and prayed before the God of heaven" (Nehemiah 1:4). Reports of tragedy may constitute God's call to pray in the Spirit.

Direction for prayer in the Spirit can come from a strong impression, possibly through a word of knowledge or a dream. The Holy Spirit is sovereign, and direction comes at His discretion. Our responsibility is to be so sensitive to the Spirit that we become His instruments in effective prayer.

The Holy Spirit's prompting is also an important aspect of praying in the Spirit. This kind of prayer includes the activity of both the believer and the Holy Spirit, who impresses the believer to intercede.

As in any spiritual activity, we can become so engrossed with even church-related responsibilities that our sensitivity is dulled, and we fail to respond to the Spirit's prompting. On the other hand, it is possible to become presumptuous and develop a "God told me" complex with self-exaltation as a by-product. Learning to cooperate with the Spirit in prayer is a lifelong process which should always have priority.

Prayer prompted by the Spirit may be in the language

with which we are acquainted or in an unlearned language. Paul wrote, "What is it then? I will pray with the spirit, and I will pray with the understanding also" (1 Corinthians 14:15). Prayer inspired by the Spirit might be groanings which cannot be uttered (Romans 8:26,27). John Bunyan wrote: "When thou prayest, rather let thy heart be without words than thy words without heart."

Need of Prayer in the Spirit

Here are three reasons we should ask the Holy Spirit to teach us to pray in the Spirit.

First, we need to recognize there are times we don't know how to pray or what we should pray for. The apostle Paul called it an infirmity for which prayer in the Spirit is the solution (Romans 8:26). Rather than being frustrated by the complexities of life, the believer can let the Holy Spirit intercede through him or her, according to the will of God (v.27).

Second, we wrestle against the powers of darkness. Paul wrote, "For we wrestle not against flesh and blood, but against principalities, against powers, against the rulers of the darkness of this world, against spiritual wickedness in high places" (Ephesians 6:12). Paul gave the solution: "Praying always with all prayer and supplication in the Spirit" (v.18).

Third, endtime conditions make prayer in the Spirit an urgent necessity. Satan knows his time is limited. An acceleration of demonic activity can be expected. Jude wrote of "mockers in the last time, who should walk after their own ungodly lusts" (Jude 18; see also 2 Timothy 3:1-9). Satan is using every means possible to hinder the work of God.

God's people, however, are not helpless before this onslaught of evil activity. Jude reminded believers of the solution: "But ye, beloved, building up yourselves on your most holy faith, praying in the Holy Ghost" (Jude 20).

Triumph of Prayer in the Spirit

While there is hostility in the world today against the principles of God's Word, we can be encouraged by the victory which results from prayer in the Spirit. God has not called any believer to a life of defeat, but rather to be more than a conqueror through prayer directed and prompted by the Holy Spirit.

Elijah prayed in the Spirit when he was surrounded by the forces of hell, and fire fell from heaven (1 Kings 18:37,38).

God foreknew the conditions the Church would face in the endtime, and He provided supernatural power for this time. In the last days perilous times can be expected, but in the last days God will pour out His Spirit copiously (Acts 2:17). Just as the apostles through prayer in the Spirit were empowered and emboldened to witness in the face of hostility (Acts 4:23-33), the Church today can expect a supernatural anointing in prayer, making it possible to witness effectively to this generation.

As we evaluate our personal abilities, we are often overwhelmed with a sense of inadequacy. But if we allow the Spirit to teach us to pray in the Spirit, God will take us in our weakness and accomplish great victories.

Sometimes we become so engrossed in activities that we lose the desire to pray as God would have us pray. R.A. Torrey said: "Oftentimes when we come to God in prayer, we do not feel like praying. What shall one do in such a case? Cease praying until he does feel like it? Not at all. When we feel least like praying is the time when we most need to pray. We should wait quietly before God and tell Him how cold and prayerless our hearts are, and look up to Him and trust Him and expect Him to send the Holy Spirit to warm our hearts and draw them out in prayer. It will not be long before the flow of the Spirit's presence will fill our hearts, and we will begin to pray with freedom, directness, earnestness and power."

Holy Spirit, teach us to pray in the Spirit.

Hardy W. Steinberg (1918-93) was national director of the Division of Christian Education for the Assemblies of God (1972-86).

20

HOW CAN THE INFILLING OF THE SPIRIT BE EXPLAINED?

By Dean Merrill

My son was about 8 or 9 when he began noticing his father's appreciation for exotic cars. He had listened to me exclaim, "Ooh, look at that Mercedes 300 SL!" enough times to learn that not all automobiles were created equal.

One day he inquired, "Dad, what's so great about a Mercedes?"

"Oh, my—they're just one of the best cars in the world, Nathan. Built in Germany—they're great."

He looked puzzled. "Do they go faster than any other car?" he asked.

"No, I don't suppose so. They're just really well made."

"Well," he said, looking out the window, "they have four wheels, doors, and windows like other cars, right? What's so great about them?"

"Uh, well …" It was becoming apparent I didn't know enough about a Mercedes to state its specific merits. All I could do was spout the superlatives: "wonderful … terrific

... great ... incredible."

This exchange with my son reminded me of something similar in the spiritual world. How many of us Pentecostals can clearly explain what's so great about the infilling of the Holy Spirit? We're often enthusiastic: "Oh, it's a tremendous blessing in my life ... a wonderful experience ... something that just means so much to me ... it's fantastic."

New Christians or friends from other church backgrounds scratch their heads thinking, *Yes, but what is it? Define what you mean. What exactly are you talking about?* We have traditionally been long on sales pitch and short on definition.

Feeling the Chill

In Robert Boyd Munger's booklet, *My Heart: Christ's Home*, he compares the Christian's daily life to welcoming Christ into the various rooms of a house: the dining room (appetites and desires), the workshop (talents and skills), the study (books and magazines), the family room (friendships and amusements), and even the hall closet (deep, dark secrets).

Imagine coming back to your home after a winter vacation. The rooms are cold because you turned down the thermostat before leaving; you wanted to save heat. Now you immediately turn the dial back up, and within 15 minutes or so the house will be filled with warmth.

In the Old Testament the word for Spirit is the Hebrew *ruach*—wind, breath, spirit. Sometimes the translators debate which to use. For example, in Genesis 1:2 should it say the "wind" of God moved upon the waters, or the "Spirit" of God? *Ruach* fits either one.

In New Testament Greek the same thing occurs. *Pneuma* means wind, breath, spirit. Thus in English if you have pneumonia, your wind isn't moving very well. Your dentist uses a pneumatic drill—a drill that runs on forced air. No wonder Jesus on Easter night "breathed on them and said, 'Receive the Holy Spirit' " (John 20:22*).

---

*Scripture references in this chapter are from the New International Version.

Warming the House

So the infilling of the Spirit lets the warm air of the Spirit blow through all the rooms of my house—the various roles and aspects of my life. The Holy Spirit dispels the cold and replaces the chill with life and warmth and movement. Instead of huddling in discomfort and apprehension, I am free to move, stretch, reach out, and create.

The furnace first kicked on in my life as a young boy on the front row of First Assembly of God, Waxahachie, Texas. I will always cherish that Tuesday night when a visiting Bible teacher, J.B. Stiles, laid his hand on my head, said a few words, and I began to quietly speak in an unknown language. That was the start.

My house wasn't much to fill then. As a grade schooler I suppose you could say there was a room marked "family member" (youngest) and another room marked "student in second grade."

Since then I've added lots of rooms. The remodelers have added more space for "husband, father, churchman, writer/editor, manager at the office, and citizen."

If you ask, "Dean, are you filled with the Spirit?" I could tell you about that night in Waxahachie, but what about now? That would make me face the question of whether I've allowed heating ducts to be installed in the new areas of my life, and whether the warmth of the Spirit is filling those rooms today. How do I relate to my wife and children? How do I treat my secretary? How do I talk about my co-workers or my pastor? How am I reaching out to people who don't know Jesus?

Sometimes a piece of furniture can be carelessly placed over a room's heating vent, blocking the flow of warm air. The same thing can happen spiritually whenever I refuse to let the Spirit's breath invade a given area of my life. Heat is available, but my room remains cold.

Maintaining the Flow

All this amounts to a definition of infilling that is dynamic rather than static. The apostle Paul in Ephesians 5:18 did not write, "Get filled with the Spirit," as if it were a one-time achievement. Greek scholars say he wrote, "Be always being filled." In other words, start up the furnace fan every day, every hour. The chill of the world is ever present, wanting to freeze our relationships with God and one another. Only a constant flow of Spirit warmth will keep us healthy and limber.

What is the role of speaking in tongues? It is the whoosh of the divine Wind, the sound that accompanies the Spirit's invasion. It's not the heat itself, but rather the noise of its activity.

The chill of winter in Colorado is occasionally relieved by the sudden arrival of a chinook—a warm, dry wind coming over the mountains from the west. It's also known as the snow eater, because it can melt snowbanks almost before your eyes. In Rapid City, South Dakota, a winter chinook once raised the temperature 44 degrees in 15 minutes.

My life—and yours—needs a chinook of the Holy Spirit from time to time. What causes such an invasion? Robert Tuttle Jr., in his book, *Someone Out There Needs Me*, writes, "Most of us know that wind blows from high pressure to low pressure, to the point of least resistance. Likewise, the Holy Spirit ... moves from high pressure to low pressure, to the point of least resistance, to the 'I give up.' "

May the warm airflow of the Spirit move freely throughout the rooms of our lives, causing love, joy, gentleness, kindness and all the other results listed in Galatians 5. Then we can indeed claim to be Spirit-filled—and confidently explain what it means to others.

Dean Merrill is a member of Living Springs Worship Centre (Assemblies of God), Colorado Springs, Colorado, and is vice president and publisher of International Bible Society.

21

CAN CHILDREN RECEIVE THE BAPTISM?

By Richard L. Dresselhaus

The prayer room is packed with boys and girls who have responded to the camp evangelist's invitation, "Come and be filled with the Spirit." One by one, children begin to speak in tongues. Adult counselors are thrilled at the outpouring of the Holy Spirit.

A dozen years pass, and a young lady sits in a pastor's study and confesses that 12 years earlier she was one of those children, but in reality she had not received the baptism in the Holy Spirit. The guilt of claiming a spiritual experience that was not authentic has blighted her spiritual growth.

How tragic that at times enthusiastic and sincere adults have failed to teach the biblical truths about the baptism in the Spirit and instead have encouraged an experiential encounter with the Holy Spirit that is not grounded in the Scriptures.

Focus on the Problem

Children should be led to Christ as Savior as soon as they are able to comprehend that truth. And instruction on the

105

baptism in the Holy Spirit should follow in sequence.

The question is not whether children can or should receive the baptism in the Spirit. It is a question of their being properly taught. Experience is not the final test for truth and reality. The Word alone is the ground out of which every experience with God must rise. Children must be taught what the Bible says about the baptism in the Spirit. In the event a child receives the Baptism without being carefully taught, an adult should quickly undergird that experience with the Word of God.

Satan is good at snatching unsecured experiences from the sincere. His question always strikes at the point of authority: "Has God spoken?" Only the Word of God can rise against the accuser and level his accusation.

Truth Explained

What do children need to understand as they wait before God to be filled with His Spirit?

Scriptural setting. Children must see that the Old Testament prophets foresaw this outpouring, and the New Testament records its fulfillment. And there is no indication that the blessing ceased at the close of the Apostolic Era. The following Scriptures are helpful: Joel 2:28,29; Luke 24:44-53; John 1:29-34; Acts 2:1-4; 10:44-48; 19:1-7; 1 Corinthians 12:4-11; 14:1,2.

Analogy principle. Since God's dealings with mankind are progressive and dynamic, we may rightly expect that the Spirit will fall in our day as He did during New Testament days.

Children should be taught to receive the fullness of the Spirit in the same fashion as the early believers.

Place of tongues. Three distinct uses of tongues are seen in the New Testament: Speaking in tongues as an evidence of the infilling of the Spirit (Acts 2:4; 10:46; 19:6); tongues as a part of the believer's devotional life (1 Corinthians 14:2); tongues as used in the assembly, to be followed by an interpretation (1 Corinthians 12:10).

Children should know that they may expect to speak in tongues as an evidence, or first physical sign, of the baptism in the Spirit.

Value of the baptism in the Spirit. Why should children be encouraged to receive the baptism in the Spirit? The baptism in the Spirit is not a toy to be entertained with, nor is it intended to be a stamp of spiritual achievement, nor is it sure proof of spiritual power. The Lord fills His children with His Spirit so His likeness may be in more perfect evidence.

The Spirit is given to manifest Jesus—to make the believer more like Christ. The baptism in the Spirit brings His children low before the Cross and prompts their hearts to rejoice.

Truth Experienced

In love and with spiritual sensitivity, we can bring children face to face with the truth of the baptism in the Holy Spirit as set forth in the Scriptures. But what should they do with that knowledge? Not until they act in faith and obedience upon what has been learned will the experience become personal.

Following are suggestions to help guide a child to the experience of the baptism in the Spirit:

Be certain the child understands that the baptism in the Spirit cannot be earned, nor is it bestowed according to personal merit or achievement. It is a benefit of God's grace. As such, it is a pure gift. Help the child see that the Heavenly Father desires to give a priceless gift as a token of His love.

Remember there is no technique to follow in helping a child receive the baptism in the Spirit. Asking a child to make sounds in a repetitious fashion, or coaching a child into a recitation of tongues-like words, or encouraging emotional responses detract from the sovereignty of God. The Spirit is the bearer of all truth. He is great enough to prompt an utterance in a heavenly language.

Be aware that fear inevitably accompanies the unknown. A child is hesitant to open himself or herself to an experience that seems unusual and strange. A wise counselor will take time to explain that God loves us so much that He desires our praise. And to make our praise more personal He gives us a language of His choosing to express it.

Do not set a chronological age as the appropriate time for a child to be encouraged to receive the baptism in the Spirit. Each child is different in background, Bible knowledge, intelligence level, and spiritual development. The important matter is the ability to comprehend the biblical truth and principles that relate to the baptism in the Spirit.

Recognize the sovereignty of the Spirit. Let the Spirit move as He chooses in the heart of a child. Overzealous counselors can force a testimony before the Spirit has finished His work.

There is no prescribed pattern by which the Spirit works. For some children, great joy will be evident; to others a deep peace will come; yet others will sense an urge to share Christ.

Truth in Evidence

Children who receive the baptism in the Spirit must be taught that the way is now open for a life of spiritual fullness and fruitfulness. The Spirit in them will produce the very attributes of Jesus Christ—love, joy, peace, long-suffering, gentleness, goodness, faith, meekness, and temperance. And this is what the world needs to see.

Our children are a sacred charge. They deserve our best efforts and our continual prayers.

Richard L. Dresselhaus, D.Min., is pastor of First Assembly of God in San Diego, California, and is an executive presbyter of the Assemblies of God.

22

CAN THE HOLY SPIRIT BRING PEOPLE TOGETHER?

By James K. Bridges

When Luke, the physician, wrote The Acts of the Apostles, he used the adverb *homothumadon*, which is translated "with one accord," 11 times. The word is used only one other time in the New Testament. It is Luke's special word meaning more than just getting together in one place; it involves unity of mind, spirit, and purpose.

J. Roswell Flower, former general secretary of the Assemblies of God, pointed out that *homothumadon* had special significance to Luke: "He used it to mean more than agreement of ideas. One-accordness is a flowing together of the spirits of men to one purpose until it becomes a passion."

As we observe how Luke used the word, we understand the power of such a passion.

Prayer Accord

From the beginning, Christ's followers "continued with one accord in prayer and supplication" (1:14), maintaining

109

close communion with the risen Lord. They understood that strength to overcome persecution and to boldly proclaim the gospel of Christ would come through prayer. So after being released from arrest by the religious authorities, "they raised their voice to God with one accord" (4:24), and "when they had prayed, the place where they were assembled together was shaken; and they were all filled with the Holy Spirit and they spoke the word of God with boldness" (4:31).

The church today must experience the prayer accord that characterized the Early Church.

Pentecost Accord

As the disciples prepared for the coming of the Holy Spirit on the Day of Pentecost, "they were all with one accord in one place" (2:1). This attitude of heart and mind is essential to receiving the baptism in the Holy Spirit. It is also essential for the Church to live in this unity in order for the work of God to be accomplished. When Luke reported signs and wonders along with believers being added to the Lord, he connected it to this statement: "They were all with one accord in Solomon's porch" (5:12).

Pentecost accord is essential for a Pentecostal church to retain its Pentecostal heritage.

Power Accord

Luke described the Pentecostal believers as "continuing daily with one accord" (2:46). Through the power of the Spirit, the disciples "continued steadfastly in the apostles' doctrine and fellowship, in the breaking of bread, and in prayers" (2:42). They found staying power that supported them in their mission to declare what God had done in Christ. They found that, when they "assembled with one accord" (15:25) to conduct their business, they gained wisdom and resolution "which seemed good to the Holy Spirit and to them" (15:28). As they continued in the sound teaching of the apostles, the unity of the Spirit led them into the unity of the faith. The Early Church found keeping power that prevented them from being swept away with every wind of doctrine.

Without power accord, the Pentecostal believer will never fulfill a Pentecostal ministry.

Luke gave us a picture of unity among the idol worshipers at Ephesus when he noted that they "rushed into the theater with one accord" (19:29) and "all with one voice cried out for about two hours, 'Great is Diana of the Ephesians!' " (19:34). He gave another example when the Jews attacked Stephen "with one accord" (7:57) and "gnashed at him with their teeth" (7:54), stoning him to death. But this is destructive unity.

By contrast, when the people of Samaria "with one accord heeded the things spoken by Philip" (8:6), a great revival occurred and the city was full of joy. The result of such unity was that many were converted and received the Holy Spirit baptism (8:14,15).

Through the Holy Spirit, Luke has given us a special word that is the key to Pentecostal experience and Pentecostal ministry. Let us seek to be "with one accord."

James K. Bridges is general treasurer of the Assemblies of God.

Appendix

MORE QUESTIONS AND ANSWERS ABOUT THE HOLY SPIRIT

Do Christians receive the Holy Spirit when they are saved? If so, how is that experience different from the baptism in the Holy Spirit?

Yes, when persons accept Christ, the Holy Spirit begins a great work in their lives. The Spirit convicts them of sin, convinces them of righteousness, and dwells within them (John 6:44; 14:17; Roman 8:9; 1 Corinthians 12:13). No one becomes a Christian without this gracious work of the Holy Spirit.

However, there is an additional and distinct ministry of the Holy Spirit called the baptism in the Holy Spirit. The Baptism is an empowering gift from God the Father that is promised to every believer (Matthew 3:11; Luke 11:13; 24:49; Acts 2:33,38). It helps the Christian to live a holy life and also brings a new devotional attachment to Jesus Christ, making Him very real and precious. The primary purpose of the Baptism is to give greater power for witnessing (Acts 1:8). Other benefits include a greater joy in spiritual service and a heightened sense of one's mission to the world.

Can a person receive eternal life in heaven without the baptism in the Holy Spirit? If so, why should we be baptized in the Spirit?

Receiving eternal life does not depend on being baptized in the Holy Spirit, for salvation is by grace through faith alone (Habakkuk 2:4; John 6:28,29; Galatians 3:6; 5:6; Ephesians 2:8). It is a gift purchased for us by Christ when He was crucified. All we have to do is accept the gift. Just as the repentant thief on the cross next to Jesus was assured of entering paradise that very day, we too are assured a place in heaven with the Father if we believe in Jesus Christ. It is most unfortunate that some have said, "Unless you have spoken in tongues you will not go to heaven." This is contrary to the Scriptures.

At the same time, the Bible does tell us that Christ commanded His first followers to wait for the Holy Spirit to come upon them (Luke 24:49; Acts 1:8). The Bible commands us to "be filled with the Spirit" (Ephesians 5:18*). This personal encounter with the Holy Spirit should be sought and cherished by every believer. With it comes a new and fuller dimension of spiritual understanding and a flow of spiritual gifts (1 Corinthians 2:9-13).

Do we play a role as to whether or not tongues and other gifts will operate in the church?

Human availability has always been an essential part of the unfolding of God's plan. Throughout Scripture there is an obvious blending of God's sovereign purposes and people's availability in implementing those purposes. While this interrelationship is impossible to fully comprehend, it is consistently recorded in the Bible.

* Scripture references are from the New International Version.

Spiritual gifts operate only with human availability. While the gifts are supernatural both in source and operation, they require willing and obedient hearts through which they might find expression. Jesus commanded His disciples to wait in Jerusalem until they had been "clothed with power from on high" (Luke 24:49). It was not until they had placed themselves at the Spirit's disposal that they were "filled with the Holy Spirit and began to speak in other tongues as the Spirit enabled them" (Acts 2:4).

This interrelationship between the Holy Spirit and human availability can be expressed by the following progression: The believer must (1) have a clear understanding of the biblical base for promised gifts; (2) be touched in his or her heart with a desire for the gifts to flow; (3) be willing to submit to the inner sense that the Spirit is seeking expression; and (4) offer to the Holy Spirit his or her heart, emotions, will, and voice by which those gifts may operate. The key is obedient availability coupled with a sincere desire to please God.

Can a person be filled with the Holy Spirit without speaking in tongues?

On the Day of Pentecost the Holy Spirit fell upon the assembled believers and "all of them were filled with the Holy Spirit and began to speak in other tongues" (Acts 2:4). Later, as Peter was preaching at the house of Cornelius, "the Holy Spirit came on all who heard the message" and they were "speaking in tongues and praising God" (Acts 10:44,46). Again, as the apostle Paul was ministering to the Ephesian disciples, "the Holy Spirit came on them, and they spoke in tongues and prophesied" (Acts 19:6). It is evident also that Paul himself was filled with the Holy Spirit (Acts 9:17) and spoke in tongues (1 Corinthians 14:18). These Scriptures clearly show that speaking in tongues is the initial physical evidence of being baptized in the Holy Spirit.

When the early believers were filled, they spoke in other tongues, and the same holds true today. Millions of believers worldwide share the exact testimony: when they initially were baptized in the Holy Spirit, they spoke in unknown tongues. The prophecy of Joel 2:28,29, cited by Peter in Acts 2:16,17, links today's Spirit-filled believers with those who were filled with the Spirit on the Day of Pentecost.

We affirm and teach these truths because they are based upon the pattern from God's Word. We do not look upon speaking in tongues as a proof of superior spirituality. It is simply a precious promise written in God's Word and fulfilled in our lives. To ignore it is to miss a great blessing and come short of the New Testament pattern.

All who are hungry for the "filling" should be encouraged to trust the Lord for the overflowing evidence of that "filling," namely, speaking in other tongues.

Who should be baptized in the Holy Spirit?

When the believers were assembled in prayer on the Day of Pentecost, "All of them were filled with the Holy Spirit and began to speak in other tongues as the Spirit enabled them" (Acts 2:4). Not one was left out. It was not just the apostles who were filled, but all the men and all the women in that company of 120 persons. Then the apostle Peter addressed the onlookers and told them that they should be filled. He said, "The promise is for you and your children and for all who are far off—for all whom the Lord our God will call" (Acts 2:39).

As Peter said, the baptism in the Holy Spirit is for every believer in every generation.

When an individual is seeking the baptism in the Holy Spirit, can anything be done to prepare his/her life or environment that will quicken the infilling?

One thing the believer should do is to seek the Baptizer rather than the Baptism. It is Jesus who baptizes believers in the Holy Spirit. Seekers should focus their attention on Him rather than on an experience.

There are other steps that, if taken, will assist seekers. (1) Understand that the baptism in the Holy Spirit is a gift from God. It should be received with gratitude and giving of thanks to the Giver. It cannot be earned or merited. It can only be accepted with an open and willing heart. (2) Be fully persuaded that the baptism in the Holy Spirit is both biblical and doctrinally correct. (3) Confess any known sins in your life and resolve to live a righteous life with God's help. (4) Begin to worship the Lord with expressions of praise and adoration. (5) Express to the Lord, who is the Baptizer, a desire to be filled with the Holy Spirit for His glory. (6) Yield to any deep "welling up" within your spirit and allow that inner surge to break through in expressions of worship, praise, and adoration in a language unknown to you but meaningful to God.

Is tongues the only evidence of the infilling of the Holy Spirit? Will there be any significant changes in one's attitudes and actions after being baptized in the Spirit?

The first physical sign of the infilling of the Spirit is speaking in tongues. This is the one physical sign that is consistent in its recurrence. However, the Baptism is not a goal but a gateway. It is a door to Spirit-filled living. It marks a beginning, not an end. Speaking in tongues is but the initial evidence and is to be followed by all the evidences of Christlikeness that mark a consistent Spirit-filled life.

The apostle Paul described this wonderful life in the Spirit in Galatians 5:22,23: "The fruit of the Spirit is love, joy, peace, patience, kindness, goodness, faithfulness, gentleness and self-control."

It is a life to be lived, not just an experience to be remembered. Some have missed this essential distinction. They have been satisfied to recall that wonderful moment when the Holy Spirit came in His fullness and they magnified the Lord in other tongues. Failure to progress beyond that point is a tragedy. The question is not only, "Have you been filled?" but "How have you lived since you were filled?" The apostle Paul wrote, "Since we live by the Spirit, let us keep in step with the Spirit" (Galatians 5:25). The baptism in the Holy Spirit is the introduction to a victorious Christian life in the Spirit.

Adapted from *The Assemblies of God—Our Distinctive Doctrine...The Baptism in the Holy Spirit*, an information piece produced by the Office of Public Relations of the General Council of the Assemblies of God.

For additional copies of *Questions and Answers about the Holy Spirit*, call:

Gospel Publishing House
1 (800) 641-4310
Please request product number 02-3032.

Other PE Books available:
Strategies for Victorious Christian Living
(product number 02-1032)
Family: How To Have a Healthy Christian Home
(product number 02-1034)

Visit our website at pe.ag.org

To subscribe to the *Pentecostal Evangel* magazine, call 1 (800) 641-4310.